Ken Duncum grew up in Rotorua and has been writing for theatre for over twenty-five years.

In the 1980s he worked with Rebecca Rodden. Their full-length play, *Jism* (1989) was named Play of the Year by the *Dominion*. Ken's subsequent work for screen and stage includes the plays *Blue Sky Boys* (Best New Zealand Play 1990), *Flipside* (Chapman Tripp Award for Production of the Year 2000), *Trick of the Light* (Best New Zealand Play 2002), and *Cherish* (Best New Zealand Play 2003), as well as scripts for major television shows like *Duggan* and *Cover Story* (Best Script, TV Drama, Film and TV Awards 1997). *Flipside*, *Trick of the Light* and *Horseplay* were published by Victoria University Press in 2005 as *Plays 1: Small Towns & Sea*. His later plays include *Picture Perfect* (2006) and an adaptation of F. Scott Fitzgerald's *The Great Gatsby* (2009).

In September 2001 Ken was the inaugural recipient of the Michael Hirschfeld Memorial Writing Award, and in 2002 he began as the Michael Hirschfeld Director of Scriptwriting, coordinating the MA in scriptwriting at Victoria University's International Institute of Modern Letters.

The introductions to the plays in this volume were written in Menton, France during his time there as winner of the 2010 NZ Post Katherine Mansfield Prize, New Zealand's most prestigious literary award.

PLAYS 2: LONDON CALLING

Blue Sky Boys

John, I'm Only Dancing

Waterloo Sunset

Ken Duncum

VICTORIA UNIVERSITY PRESS

VICTORIA UNIVERSITY PRESS
Victoria University of Wellington
PO Box 600 Wellington
vuw.ac.nz/vup

National Library of New Zealand Cataloguing-in-Publication Data

Duncum, Ken, 1959-
Plays 2 : London calling / Ken Duncum.
ISBN 978-0-86473-684-0
I. Title.
NZ822.3—dc 22

Printed by PrintStop, Wellington

CONTENTS

INTRODUCTION

London is a mythical place – perhaps even more so now that I've actually been there. On the summer evening that I finally reached the city of that name, a quarter century after I thought I would, I found myself floating through a haze of jet-lag and euphoria towards the dome of St Paul's. Laid out against a sunset sky of Turner-esque cloudscape I could only think how much it looked like every painting I'd ever seen of it. I tried to shake the sensation off, wanting to 'be here now', but as I got closer in the fading light the cathedral itself started to resemble a giant drawing. I squinted, expecting at any moment my idea of this iconic building to drop away like a curtain, allowing the reality to be seen. The opposite happened. As I neared it, the familiar outline stubbornly became more drawing-like. What was wrong with me that I couldn't see it as it was, only as the two-dimensional representations I'd known before? Had I left this whole London thing too late? Just how hopelessly colonial was I?

I walked right up to the cathedral.

It was a drawing.

They were doing restoration work and had draped the entire side in plastic printed with one of Christopher Wren's original architectural diagrams. Life-size.

It remains the largest and most perfect metaphor I've ever seen.

The three plays in this book I think of as the 'music plays'. If you'd asked me ten years ago, I would have said they were about the intersection of popular overseas music culture with New Zealand society, each of them showing a slice of Kiwi kids seeking an identity and a relationship to the world through different ways of dressing, talking, posing and thinking delivered to them through music. British music. The paradox of us looking to another culture to tell us who we are.

And that is indeed one connecting element. But increasingly clear to me, as I walk away from these plays, is another – that their central characters are all struggling to make a present in the overwhelming shadow of their past; the blame, pain and recrimination that still attaches to them.

And in each case, in each relationship, out of struggle and exhaustion comes hope. And kindness. Which – in the end – are the clothes that love wears. Don and Phil Everly find a moment for the magic to happen one more time, John Jamieson loses in love but triumphs in fantasy, Julie and Terry pass through the fire but will stay together.

Underneath the songs performed and referenced in them, I hear another music stitching these plays together – a harmony, sweet and stinging, of loss and redemption.

Ken Duncum
2011

BLUE SKY BOYS

INTRODUCTION

One day in Courtenay Place I met Michael Galvin, who asked me what was happening with 'that play about the Everly Brothers'. I said I was going to finish it and try to get it on. He said how about finishing it for him and Tim, who were soon to graduate from Drama School? I remember looking at him and saying, 'Can you sing and play guitar?'

One evening some time later – but not too much time, as memory telescopes the events of twenty years ago – I remember turning the corner into Courtenay Place, well within sight of the kerb on which I'd had that conversation with Michael, to find the front of the St James Theatre brilliantly lit up and a buzzing expectant crowd stretching out into the street. Cars were having to go round them. A huge banner on the front of the theatre read '*Blue Sky Boys* by Ken Duncum'.

Rock'n'Roll!

There are actually a lot of memories connected with *Blue Sky Boys* – and I can link them up in many different orders and directions. One of the most central is the cartoon cover of a 'best of' album of the Everly Brothers which has repaid its five-dollar cost in Silvio's or Record Preservation many times over. Those were the second-hand record shops in Cuba Street I would visit at least every Friday night to pick over the new arrivals and scrutinise their black plastic for scratches under the fluorescent lights.

I've never learnt an instrument – apart from unfortunate incidents with recorder and ukulele at primary school – but I love music. Rock'n'roll, pop music, rock music, punk, new wave – records were desperately important to me and I became a collector of sorts. 'Of sorts' because I didn't have the money to buy new or chase up rarities – I just needed music, and it was a constant unfolding discovery for me.

I came to it first through my brother, who was two years older and was the first to find connection and inspiration through the records of the time. *Led Zeppelin II* and *III*, Black Sabbath's *Paranoid*, the

Doors' *Weird Scenes Inside the Gold Mine*, *Cosmo's Factory* by Creedence Clearwater Revival, one solitary Beatles album (*Let It Be*), *Goats Head Soup* and *Their Satanic Majesties Request* by the Rolling Stones, *Death Walks Behind You* by Atomic Rooster, Donovan's *Cosmic Wheels* – and many other titles (and images of covers) which, though played to pieces on the stereogram in our shared room, find themselves a little more obscured by history: Blue Cheer, Captain Beyond, Juicy Lucy, Warhorse, *Vertigo Annual*, The Temptations' *Wings of Love* album …

As you can no doubt guess by now, I could go on. Suffice to say that my brother introduced me to music as I understood it then and still understand it – and he bought me my first LP, *Dark Side of the Moon*, gatefold with two free posters. You will also not be surprised to learn that I still have it.

As music rolled forward I did my best to keep up with it, but my interest also extended backwards to songs that were written and recorded by bands and artists while I was starting school, or learning to walk, or not even born. When I was fifteen I spent my wages from a week-long painting job on a copy of artist Guy Peellaert's book *Rock Dreams*, which gave me an evocative and endlessly-thumbed illuminated manuscript of the roots of rock music from the early fifties on up. It also gave me a map of discovery which took me many years to trace.

This process accelerated when I met my girlfriend, later mother of my children, who was ten years older than me. We bonded over the Beatles, and she introduced me to the Walker Brothers, Scott Walker and Nina Simone. I would look up from the record racks and see her, as we met in Silvio's every Friday night before catching the bus home. She told me stories of the sixties, particularly her experiences as a young teen when the Beatles came to Wellington, and later at Rolling Stones and Walker Brothers concerts in the Town Hall. In the end it seemed appropriate to give her Christian and middle names to the characters of the girls in *Blue Sky Boys*, though her escapades were far more innocent and the outcomes happier than what befalls Jillian and Fran in the play.

So, somewhere past the mid-point of the eighties I bought this Everly Brothers record – and found out just how good they were. For six years from 1957 they were unequivocally the biggest band in the world, before the Beatles descended like a cleaver and they never had another hit in their home country of the United States. Britain, however, kept the faith and gave them a UK hit with their comeback single 'The Price of Love'. Besides the Beatles and the English Invasion, there was much for the Everlys to come back from – Don's drug-and-fame-driven breakdown, raging creative and personal conflicts between the brothers – like all good dramas the internal tensions were equal to the external ones. And that was the lone other fact I knew as I listened to the music and traced their rise and fall through the table of chart placings on the back of the album: they didn't get on. For all the beautiful preternatural harmony of their voices, their backstage personalities were in violent disharmony. But there was no escape, their singing manacled them and their destinies together as surely as if they were conjoined (curiously enough, the main characters in the play I was writing at the time were Siamese twin sisters).

I can remember standing in the kitchen of our house in Miramar, waving the record sleeve of *Walk Right Back With The Everlys: 20 Golden Hits* – with its cartoon-strip cover stringing all the song titles together into a brightly-coloured fifties-drenched story of sunshine and love gained and lost – and saying, 'You know, someone should write a play about this.'

Or, rather, getting halfway through that sentence and stopping as I realised that in fact I fancied myself as a playwright. That I had written plays and wanted to write more plays. Eureka moment.

And a eureka moment for more than just *Blue Sky Boys*. In that instant worlds collided – my passion for music, how music reflected and refracted the people and the places it came from, and my passion for theatre which did the same thing.

I said, 'No. I should. I should write a play about the Everly Brothers.' So I did.

And I wrote it about a lot more besides. About Wellington and New Zealand at a moment of huge cultural change (in my history book at least), about the lifeline music can be, the tension between dreams and reality, between art and commerce, about the nature of the creative act, loss of innocence, the dangers of confusing the singer with the song and the closeness of love and hate.

And I felt – as I wrote it, and the story opened out before me, and I saw how and where the songs would fit – that I was part of something huge and powerful. It makes me laugh now, but I thought *Blue Sky Boys* was going to utterly transform my life. Pumped up from writing spells I'd go for walks along Scorching Bay and pick which large and luxurious house on the hillside was going to be mine. (There was one with a pool, perfectly tucked into a niche in the hill . . .) I was the only one in on a secret – it was actually the first real play I'd written by myself, rather than with my writing partner Rebecca Rodden – and there in the sunlight, waves on the rocks, I could not see how this thing could fail. It was the best idea in the world.

I was still in my twenties then – and I've had quite a lot of ideas since – so now I know it was only one of the best ideas in the world.

That first ecstatic draft I submitted to the 1988 New Zealand Playwrights' Workshop organised by Playmarket and it was selected to be one of the works included in the week-long programme. In fact they created a special category for *Blue Sky Boys* – it was to be neither a reading nor a workshop but a 'presentation'. They explained that they found the script to be so complete and polished that it didn't need workshopping. I was flattered – it was the first outside acknowledgement I'd had of showing promise as a playwright – though a little perturbed to realise that in fact this meant the play would receive less rehearsal time than the workshopped plays. Despite the fact that it was drawing attention to itself by its special 'presentation' status, and that I considered it a first draft and really wanted the opportunity to work with actors and director on it.

The week was fraught – as the usual, though perhaps understandable, reasons of time and pressure were used to sideline me from the working process – but exciting too, with everyone positive and enthusiastic about the script. And the presentation on the last Saturday night of the conference went well.

I remember steering my heavily pregnant girlfriend through the crowd afterwards – and also, earlier in the week, polyurethaning our kitchen floor at one in the morning because she wanted everything ready for the baby and I was spending all my time in Upper Hutt at the conference.

After that I was distracted by the birth of my daughter Katherine, by the need to make some money and my subsequent move into writing sketch comedy for television, and by the production the following year of *Jism*, the play co-written with Rebecca featuring the Siamese twins.

Blue Sky Boys was always there – the world-beating show-in-waiting – but the next thing I clearly remember about it is that brief discussion one afternoon in Courtenay Place.

I had already known Michael Galvin and Tim Balme for some years. They were a year or two behind me in the Theatre Department at Victoria University – though I was about five years older, having come back to university to study theatre, film and writing. I'd cast Michael as the boy in the segment of *Equus* that I directed as my major piece in my last theatre course. He was fantastic – and the bolt of electricity I got from that night was what confirmed in me the desire to do more theatre in the outside world.

The following year I put a show on at Bats – directing it and paying for it myself – which was two plays co-written with Rebecca Rodden. One was a solo show for Rebecca – *Polythene Pam*. The other – *Truelove* – presented me with something of a casting problem. Everyone who read the script told me the central character was an arsehole, which was true, but I wanted the audience to empathise with him. I got put in touch with Tim Balme. Problem solved.

In fact Michael was in that play as well, as a sulky teenage monster-boy with green elephant feet. His was less a walk-on than a stomp-on part.

So those guys were around – and at that time Tim was unsure whether to pursue acting or music as his main career. He was always in a band, or a duo (with his friend Rob), writing songs and playing around town – and he was really good, I loved his music. But then Tim and Michael were both accepted into the New Zealand Drama School (it changed its name to Toi Whakaari while they were there) and were unable to be part of outside productions for two years.

But the two years rolled past, Michael and Tim became closer friends through their time at Drama School and soon were looking for something to flex their newly trained muscles, maybe something they could do together . . .

Who the director should be was obvious. Simon Bennett had also been a part of the vibrant creative community centred on the Theatre Department at Victoria University, had worked with all of us at various times (e.g. he played the father terrorised by Michael's monster-son in *Truelove*), had also graduated from the Drama School, and perhaps most importantly had, in partnership with Simon Elson, transformed Bats Theatre from a venue-for-hire into a genuine producing theatre. A vitally important theatre which continues to produce new work at a prodigious rate to this day. One of the reasons Simon decided to set up Bats was that he was aware of plays being written – by playwrights such as myself, Rebecca, Gary Henderson – which might not otherwise be produced.

The second production at the newly revamped, reshaped, repainted Bats Theatre was *Jism* (yes, that Siamese twins show again), which Simon directed. It was a success, we were thought to be punky, cutting-edge and new, and I really enjoyed working with Simon. The question naturally arose, what next? After all, there's a theatre now, showing six nights a week, demanding product year-round, so what are we doing next?

I finished that play about the Everly Brothers. In this context 'finished' means I rewrote it till I was happy with it. Or until time ran out, which is more likely.

Music rehearsals started first, and we managed to get Gary Henderson to coach Tim and Michael – which was perfect because as well as being a great musician Gary is also (of course) a brilliant playwright, so he understands drama, performance and how to shape things. On the day Gary first met with 'the boys' to work out the songs I got up from my typewriter and drove into town, walked out of the sunlight into the dimness of Bats Theatre (always a peculiar pleasure for me, walking into an empty theatre in the middle of the day) and sat in a battered seat listening and watching. Just the four of us there. I remember telling them that I wanted to see some other people working on the play for a change. But perhaps I also wanted to get some idea of whether it was going to work, whether Michael and Tim could become Phil and Don – not in the acting, I knew they could do that, but in the music, the harmonies, the guitar-playing. I left reassured, feeling that the house with the pool above Scorching Bay was almost within my grasp.

A word about the music. When I first conceived and wrote the play I had no idea whether I would be able to use the songs I wanted. I just picked, chose and joined together whatever of the Everly Brothers' back catalogue I thought would sound good and work best dramatically. When a production started to look likely I had to find out how to get performance rights. And what I discovered was astounding.

At that time – that golden time – I could get it all for a payment of 1.5% of box office. All I had to do was notify APRA of the songs we were using in the play and send them the money; they would distribute it to the music publishers. So easy! So cheap!

Vistas of plays-with-music, music-within-plays opened up before me – the eureka moment in the kitchen when my two passions collided and struck sparks off each other now seemed to have led to a career for life. My destiny was to bring drama and music (my music, the songs with meanings and cultural significance to me, that had steered my teenage and to-date adult life) together, and let each comment on the other. Possible plays cascaded into my mind. Who knew these things? Who was better equipped to do this than me? Destiny, my friend, destiny. Hand me the key to the front door of the big house.

Hah.

Here's a free-floating memory. We were in a space upstairs overlooking Courtenay Place – maybe a rehearsal room connected to the Depot Theatre? Maybe we were rehearsing for the first time with the 'full band' – i.e. Colin Kitchingman as Carl on drums, plus amplification and electric guitar? Anyway, we were working on the music and a song in the rock'n'roll bracket wasn't working. I can't remember why not or what song, but it wasn't dynamic enough. It was the song Carl's meant to kick off by suddenly appearing, drumming defiantly. The song had to take that surge of adrenaline and run with it, go even higher. And this one wasn't. But if we dropped it, what could we put in its place?

Maybe, I said, maybe . . . 'Temptation'. Everyone looked blank: What's 'Temptation'? I played the record for them. They looked at me. Why didn't you tell us about this song before? They played it. Rudimentarily. We all knew it was going to work. Except 'work' is too poverty-stricken a word for what it was going to do. You get a taste in your mouth at moments like that. I always want to cry out of sheer excitement. (For spotters: 'Temptation' was an old standard Don Everly had heard since he was a kid. His own phenomenal semi-crazed arrangement of it came to him in a dream.)

Casting was completed, the masculinity of proceedings now tempered by Stephanie Creed and Emily Perkins playing Jillian and Fran – and Peter McAllum was on board as Pete Fontaine. We started rehearsals of the play in a cold ex-church in Aro Valley – only to come to a screeching halt when early one morning fire swept through Bats Theatre, damaging the backstage areas and requiring the theatre to 'go black' for two months. After the initial shock, and the fear that Bats might never rise again, the enforced interval turned out to be to our advantage in several ways. With dressing-rooms refurbished it was a more pleasant place to work, plus we got to launch the newly saved and re-revamped Bats, and Tim and Michael did a few songs as the Everly Brothers at a variety concert at the St James Theatre organised to raise funds for the repairs – helping their confidence and providing a teaser for the play at the same time. Best of all, from my point of view, the break enabled me to do some useful rewriting based on what I'd learnt from the first week or two of rehearsal. So useful in fact that I wonder if it's not the ideal blueprint for producing a new play. Since then I've often been seized with the impulse a couple of weeks into rehearsal to shout 'Fire!' in order to buy myself some time.

Rehearsals restarted in the empty BNZ building on the corner of Lambton and Customhouse Quays. A series of long, pillared empty spaces right in the middle of town, it was perfect to rehearse in while it waited for the redevelopment that would see it become a shopping arcade. Two things I chiefly remember from there: two cops attracted by the noise strolling in on Colin Kitchingman as he practiced the drums late one night. They refused to believe he wasn't illegally living in the space, producing the rolled-up sleeping bag he was using to deaden the bass drum as evidence. Or maybe they just didn't have much on that night. The other memory is of my daughter Katherine and her mother coming into rehearsal one afternoon. She was about eighteen months old and was a bit perturbed to find strange men shouting at each other while we sat two metres away seemingly too afraid to make a sound. She cried. Understandably. I took her to play amongst the pillars and worn industrial carpet of the ghost bank as her mum gathered the company at her feet and told them stories of what it was like to be a teen in Wellington in the mid-sixties.

Two asides. When I got the idea for a play about the Everly Brothers playing Wellington on the same historic night as the Beatles, I didn't know whether they had ever actually visited these shores. Coincidentally, as I worked on the play I uncovered traces of their footprints. First in an interview I read with Bill Manhire (my creative writing teacher at Victoria University) where he casually mentioned attending concerts in Dunedin by the likes of . . . and the Everly Brothers was in the list. I excitedly contacted him – he couldn't vouch for Wellington but they'd been through Dunedin more than once. Then, working my morning shift at NZ Post in Private Boxes, one of my workmates – an older woman – was whistling 'Bye Bye

Love'. I said, 'You like the Everly Brothers, Boo?' She nodded. 'Yep, saw them in the Town Hall.' Bingo!

The title. I did some research in the Public Library – the old one, before it became the Art Gallery and when you could still park outside on a one-way street that now lies under Civic Square – and read about the rich history of brother-harmony duos in country music, it being country music that the Everlys emerged from, performing from an early age on their parents' radio show. In that milieu the Everly Brothers were nothing special, it was only when they crossed over into rock'n'roll that their harmonies made them unique. That list of country acts included the Louvin Brothers, the Delmore Brothers . . . and the Blue Sky Boys. The name reverberated with me (in fact, I remembered it as the Blue Sky Brothers and thought I'd changed it to Boys so as not to indict the innocent – checking back years later, no, I'd straight-out ripped off their name) because it was so redolent of happiness, of wide open spaces and sunshine. It was the perfect name for the play – both sweet and bitterly ironic – and I could make it relate within the play to a remembered act from the Everlys' childhood which could signify to them both a warning and a reassurance. I still feel a bit guilty that I thereby (and unwittingly) made a highly respected and significant act enshrined in the Country Music Hall of Fame sound a bit second-rate. Ah well – everyone loved the title of the play and whatever else changed in the script that was always on the front page.

One more felicitous moment. My primary reference from early on was a book about the Everly Brothers which virtually leapt off the shelf of a Cuba Street bookstore at me – from their tiny selection of books on music – while I was idly browsing. Coming to me at exactly the right moment, informative, well-written, full of photos, it was also the cheapest book of its type, size and quality I had ever seen (important at the time). It and me were clearly meant to be together.

So we opened at Bats – with a fantastic grungy set designed by Helen Vasbenter – and the season sold out. I wasn't sitting alone there at midday with Gary, Michael and Tim any more – I was packed in with everyone else, with people every night sitting on the stairs up the centre aisle in contravention of the fire regulations (the good old days), probably me on those stairs so I wouldn't take a seat from a paying customer.

Apart from a generalised ecstasy, I only have one clear memory from opening night – which is the administrator from Toi Whakaari (I can only remember his first name – Paul), there to proudly support his graduates, who, as everyone milled around afterwards, came onstage and quietly and carefully tuned Colin's drums for him. You have to tune a drum? Who knew? Paul did, because he'd drummed with Deep Purple for a while, amongst others, and though he was too polite to say, he'd presumably just had to suffer the tortures of the damned during our musical segments.

Bats, Bats, Bats – it was my fourth show there, my second under the brave new banner of the Simon & Simon (Nomis Productions) Bats Theatre, and I loved the scungy old place as deeply as anyone else who'd acted, hammered, sawed, plugged, painted, stayed up till dawn fuelled by Roy's Burger Bar or otherwise enjoyed their nights there. And I loved the fact that – with full knowledge of where it would be staged – I had set the play there.

Bats had been the left-wing Unity Theatre once upon a time. It had also been (before and during WWII) a dancehall called the Savage Club. And giving an edge of bizarreness to all that went on there was the fact that the building belonged to, had been built for and still housed, the Royal Antediluvian Order of Buffaloes. The history of the place fascinated me, and squeezing the imagined events of one night in May 1964 into that history pleased me no end. Had there ever been a play that played where it was set? I supposed so but couldn't think of one. When Phil left to go meet the Beatles we all knew where he was going – out the side door, past the fire station, round the corner into Wakefield Street and down the few blocks to the Town Hall. This was our town, our history. I loved it.

And Bats was the perfect room for *Blue Sky Boys*. We were right there with them in the dressing-room, close enough to touch, to smell the angst and the Brylcreem – and when the music took off, particularly the rock'n'roll medley, right in front of us, live and sweaty, the place erupted. The walls could hardly contain it. That's my memory at least.

We had a co-op meeting before one of the early shows – I think in the very first week of the Bats run – all sitting in the first three or four rows, to discuss the possibility of extending the run to the St James Theatre for five nights. It was frighteningly soon to make such a call – Bats was tiny, the St James huge – but 'if 'twas to be' we needed to book it now. I was in favour. Better to regret having tried it than not. Tim and Michael having already been on the stage of the St James as the Everly Brothers seemed like a good omen. We went ahead.

We hyped like mad – newspapers, radio, and Tim and Michael did some 'in character' TV spots, most memorably with Belinda Todd on the original Nightline in TV3's early days when they were hungry for content and eight-minute segments were not unusual. Not so much a soundbite as a sound-five-course-meal. Completely improvised, loopy, and on the edge of crashing and burning every second. Between-the-fingers viewing for me. But outside of and perhaps despite the hype – including that huge banner on the front of the St James – the play seemed to sell itself. We played to an average audience of five hundred for five nights. That doesn't sound big time? For Wellington, for a play transferring from Bats (and we had to be the first), trust me, it was.

Two memories from those nights. I came in towards the end of the show, and walked down the long side-passageway to where we'd set up front-of-house beside the double-doors leading to the auditorium. I opened my mouth to ask how many were in tonight and was cut off by an explosion of laughter which erupted through the wall. I'd never had a moment like it before. If people had laughed at things I'd written previously, then this was five or ten times as loud and powerful. There were a lot of people in there, and they were into it. Give me more of that.

For the record, I think it was probably Pete Fontaine's 'It's the teeth' line. And front-of-house later informed me it was the biggest response they'd heard in five nights too.

The other memory comes from sitting up in the gods in the rickety and fantastic St James (before it was restored). Laurence Olivier and Vivien Leigh had played here. A play of mine was in a theatre that had boxes. Boxes!

We had a couple of guys stationed up there to work follow-spots for the music segments. They'd stand there all night on opposite sides of the gods and wiggle the spotlight a couple of times. At a certain moment in the second act, through unspoken agreement, they left their spots, came down and met at the balcony parapet, leaning over to look down on the audience. I looked at them: what are you doing? They beckoned to me. I joined them.

Up on stage, Tim as Don Everly was trying to blow his brains out while Michael as Phil goaded him to do it. It was a tense moment. Don thought the gun was fully loaded, Phil believed it was empty (since he'd unloaded it) but the audience knew that someone (Fran) had put one bullet back into the revolver. Everyone held their breath, Don sagged, he couldn't do it. Everyone relaxed. Phil took the gun, stuck it under his own chin and pulled the trigger. Something astounding happened below us as we gazed down. A gasp and a ripple of movement, a wave of physical response swept backward through the audience – something you could actually see rushed from the front rows all the way to the back, and then bounced forward again as a laugh. A laugh at themselves for getting so involved, for actually believing for an instant that someone might get shot right in front of them live onstage. I'm glad those guys called me down, because that's something that's stayed with me ever since.

And in fact I owe it to Roger Hall. During that Playwrights' Workshop where *Blue Sky Boys* was presented, Roger had been talking about playwriting craft and had lamented the fact that no one seemed to employ dramatic irony any more. We young playwrights ruminated on this for a while before, figuring I had no reputation to lose, I raised my hand. 'So . . . dramatic irony . . . what exactly is that, Roger?' 'That,' replied Roger, 'is the bomb under the table, it's when the audience knows something that the characters don't.' Hmm, I thought, how can I use that in this play? From there came the loading/unloading/reloading of the gun that created that thunderbolt moment. Thanks, Roger.

I actually hated the last night at the St James. I thought the performance was ragged, never found the right gear, and everyone should get their money back. I was kind of hard to please in those days. I wish I could say I've changed.

But overall we were a hit and that felt good. We'd taken a big chance and pulled it off. We felt like a very talented bunch of people, fortuitously come together, and *Blue Sky Boys* was a feather in all our caps. This, dear readers, is the high-water mark of the story.

Everyone got paid – not much but something. Some time later our producer realised the bill for the huge banner had been overlooked and was still outstanding (sorry for bringing it up, Dan – I know you still feel guilty about it). I paid it. It wiped out my profit on the run but maybe that was the price not of love but of ego. And after all, this was a mere bagatelle, my play and I were headed for the big time weren't we?

What next? World domination obviously. Starting with . . . Auckland. But first a rewrite. Or two.

I was unsatisfied with the script. I thought it could be better, that I could do better. When my son Jonathan was born in April of the following year, my office at home became Katherine's bedroom. I rented a space in Allen Street, actually shared it with Gary Henderson. Our landlord was a deserter from the French Foreign Legion who was living in the building illegally and was very careful about answering the door.

I bought a Macintosh computer – a cream-coloured box with a tiny black and white screen. I upgraded the RAM from 4 to 8MB, with a 52MB hard disk. Seriously tooled up. I paid far more for it than I ever have for vastly more powerful beasts since. This was pre-internet so don't even think about connection speeds. My old typewriter, that my sister had bought me in an auction from the Rotorua Police Department, and on which I'd written everything to date including last-minute blue carbon-copy rewrites, was retired honourably.

I started keeping regular office hours – and slowly, systematically, driving myself insane.

Every morning I'd drive in from Miramar, park my old Hillman Superminx in Brougham Street, Mt Victoria and walk down to the top of Courtenay Place, round the corner into Allen Street, past the skip full of discarded orange halves outside Simply Squeezed and up the stairs past the print shop to my office. Every day I'd think, this is the day I'll start writing. But every day it seemed there was just a bit more planning to do, some more notes to make, more thinking about a particularly knotty little plot complication. Just one more problem to solve first. I was convinced I had to have the structure perfect before I could start rewriting. I was convinced that there was a perfect structure, and I was close to nailing it, so close . . . I began to be lost in the maze that Roger Hall talks about in *State of the Play*. I shuffled more and more pages of scribbled notes and diagrams that stretched across pages full of shapes with tiny writing in them. I stared at blank walls and went home in a rage. Months passed.

Do not do this. Do not ever do this to yourself. As the saying goes, only writing is writing. Planning to write is not writing. Thinking about writing is not writing. Talking about writing is not writing. Standing gazing down at the stretch of Wakefield Street sidewalk where a local restaurateur died with a cop restraining him while he choked to death on a plastic bag of cocaine – and remembering how we all went to his restaurant after the last night of *Truelove/Polythene*

Pam – is not writing. No, only opening a file in MacWrite II and typing something in in order to stop that little grey cursor blinking is writing. I learnt that the hard way.

And that was just one of the things I learnt from *Blue Sky Boys*. It was wrestling with that play over a period of years, trying to make it everything I thought it could be, that taught me to write more than any other experience I've had. It's hard to divide up where a draft finishes and another draft starts, but I'd say I had at least twenty separate serious goes at that script. And for all the chasing my tail and spinning in circles till I was dizzy, it did get better and better and better. There were some people who thought I should leave it alone – some of those people were within the production – but I had a vision and I was following it.

I was gratified when halfway through rehearsals in Auckland, Michael, I think it was, said he'd looked back at the Bats/St James script and couldn't believe the difference. Yeah, it'd cost me more than a few brain cells but we were getting there.

A couple of years slipped past; that tortuous rewriting process, the business of making a living, people moving to Auckland, Michael becoming nationally known as Dr Chris Warner on *Shortland Street* – and the problem of where to find the money to put *Blue Sky Boys* on in Auckland had to be confronted.

The Maidment Theatre was the venue of choice – Steve Marshall, our lighting designer/operator from Wellington, was now working there – but how to pay the upfront costs for the Maidment? And a living wage for the actors through the rehearsal period? We had some funding from the QEII Arts Council – but we needed more.

In the end, to make it happen, I opted to put what money I had into the production. This was about $10,000, accrued through television work, and the first time in my life I'd had money in the bank. So I became an 'angel' for my own play. The two Simons, under the Nomis banner, were producers, Simon Bennett was directing again, Gary was back on board for the music, Michael and Tim playing the Everlys again, with the other four roles filled by Auckland-resident actors.

I drove up to Auckland – the Superminx was history by this time, I had a green Toyota Corona – and moved into an old house on New North Road. It had belonged to Alison Wall's (Simon Elson's then-partner) recently deceased great aunt Ruby, and seemed basically untouched since the Second World War. Pull-string lights, sumptuous lino under tattered carpet squares, rotting camellias in the overgrown garden, Big Fresh just across the road. I had one empty front bedroom, Tim had the other, Gary also had a room when he was there. I've got a great video I shot for my partner and kids of Tim giving a guided tour of the house and property. Time-slips. It's an old endangered video of a house from an even older time which no doubt doesn't exist any more.

I was there for the beginning of rehearsal, flew back to Wellington for a couple of weeks to earn some money, leaving Tim the car, then came back for the last part of rehearsals and production week.

We rehearsed in another stripped-out office space at the top of Queen Street. We had another great set for that production, and an enthusiastic cast – but it's funny, perhaps the thing I remember most clearly is the gun. We bought a proper Colt .45 replica which looked and felt like the real thing. Every guy who came into the rehearsal space would gravitate straight towards it, pick it up and play with it. I can't remember seeing a woman so much as touch it. A few years later, after the touring production, the pistol ended up going into storage in New Plymouth with the set. When I tried to get it back it turned out the storage facility had been broken into and the gun stolen. I really hope its career since then has been less rather than more dramatic.

All through rehearsal of the Auckland production there was a fly in the ointment, a constant background anxiety. It was the music rights.

I had notified APRA that we were doing a new production and looked forward to sending them the 1.5% of box office in due course. They didn't get back to me; this was before emails and their office was only open some of the time. I tried to follow up, without success, still thinking it was just a formality. Then, not long before rehearsal began, they got in touch to say there'd been some changes and APRA no longer handled rights of this kind. I would have to contact each music publishing company individually and come to an agreement firstly on whether we were allowed to use the music and secondly how much it was going to cost us.

This was a daunting task on several levels. Firstly, there were the difficulties of communication in the time we had left – in the email-less world we were living in it was by post, phone, fax or pigeon, and we quickly discovered that we were so far down the list of priorities for major US publishing companies that getting any reply at all was a challenge. Secondly, we had songs gaily scattered across a variety of music publishing companies – songs that were now dramatically locked into the show – and every reply we got to our two questions of 'Can we have the song?' and 'How much?' said 'Maybe' and 'What are the other companies charging?' No one wanted to get less than someone else, which meant whoever arbitrarily named the highest price was also setting a benchmark for the rest.

Negotiations continued at a snail's pace as our rehearsal time raced past, with us trying to explain the fundamental differences in scale, organisation and financial heft between Broadway and Auckland, between the Great White Way and the Land of the Long White Cloud.

You might ask – as I no doubt did – why we couldn't have kept our collective head down and quietly got on with it, in all probability completely unnoticed by cigar-chomping music rights moguls in Nashville and New York. Because we'd signed a contract with the Maidment Theatre guaranteeing that we had rights to all the material in the show. If that wasn't true they wouldn't take the risk of being prosecuted for copyright infringement. So we had to make it true.

Slowly we began to mosaic a deal together, while I watched my potential royalty recede like a wave. Because it all had to come out of my cut. Dramatic works garner a 10% box office royalty for their authors – that's what I'd been on in Wellington and had paid 1.5% to APRA, leaving me with 8.5% (before the banner bill came in). Now in Auckland I decided to claim 12.5%, which was the usual royalty for a musical, as some way of making up for the percentage points streaming out of my hands towards America. But by the time the counting was done, as Kenny Rogers says, the music companies were making more than me out of *Blue Sky Boys*. What had cost 1.5% of box office was now sucking up 6.5%. (We might pause here to consider that the music takes up about 1/8th of the running time of the play.) And that 6.5% agreement remains in place to this day – despite the fact that APRA shortly afterwards reverted to their original role of representing the overseas companies as a one-stop shop, ensuring a smooth, streamlined and reasonable process – because, folks, it set a precedent, and there's no going back from that. We had managed to fairly and squarely hit a brief window of chaos and anarchy in the music rights world – our timing could not have been worse.

And I'm still making it sound easier than it was. We opened without the music rights fully sorted. The day after opening night, on the afternoon of our first Sunday matinee – already not a great day in my life – Simon and Simon sat me down to explain that this second performance could very well be our last. The most-difficult-to-get-hold-of publisher had finally replied. His demand didn't mess around with the vagaries of percentage points, it was much more simple: one US dollar per seat per performance, whether that seat was filled or not – or he'd take out an injunction on our ass. The capacity of the Maidment was what, 450 seats? Let alone the outrageously bad exchange rate of the day.

'Impossible' doesn't even get near it.

I remember I was eating a burger when the Simons communicated this news to me. I was halfway through. I put it down.

There was an aspect of perfection to this disaster. A roundedness and symmetry. We'd been able to go long enough, chasing the gold ring of the music rights, just long enough for me to spend every cent of my money, just long enough to get to an uninspiring opening night and a bad review, and now we were going to be shut down before we could recoup anything, anything at all, from the quagmire.

I stared into the abyss. My burger was going cold. I picked it up, took a bite.

You've got to eat. You've got to live. Worse things happen at sea.

We didn't close early. We managed to get that music publisher to see reason, and the play ran its intended few weeks' course up until just before Christmas, getting 100–150 punters a night in the cavernous Maidment Theatre. The fact that those audiences were generally excited and enthusiastic about what they saw did go some way towards making up for other things.

But opening night – as I indicated – with by far our largest audience of everybody who was anybody in Auckland, had not gone well. Fate, nerves or the altered acoustic of a suddenly full Maidment made the performance underpowered and underwhelming. Simon and I met at intermission in the crowded foyer: what could be done, what could we do? Nothing. Trust the force. And the people on the sharp end, the ones actually up onstage doing it. And the second act was better. (Michael tells me Simon did slip backstage during the interval long enough to say 'Louder'.)

Next morning I got up early and went and bought the paper. The review was dismissive, there was an air of 'So this is what passes for good theatre in Wellington?' about it. It wasn't damning, but few people who saw it were going to rush out and buy a ticket. I couldn't quibble too much after the lacklustre performance which unfortunately we'd led with – but I also had the feeling we were the victims of our own hype. We'd sailed onto a reef in hostile territory.

I sat in the car, staring at the all-powerful *Herald* review for half an hour – at the end of which it was still the same. I got out and went for a long walk. I drove back to Aunty Ruby's house and had a cup of tea.

Gary woke to the sound of the front door slamming as I went out again. When he found the review on the kitchen table he thought he knew why. But actually that was an accident. I didn't mean to slam the door, it slipped out of my hand. I had processed and was feeling philosophical. Gary will still tell you I had a tantrum about that review.

But no, I was off at St Luke's shopping centre buying a rechargeable battery to replace the one that had died in my video camera halfway through the dress rehearsal. It was Auckland and the sun was shining – we were playing the first matinee that afternoon, we had a whole season ahead of us, the performances would re-find the magic they had in rehearsals, we'd claw our way back through positive word of mouth. I picked up my tripod, headed for the Maidment for the matinee, got a burger on the way in. Simon and Simon not looking too happy, need a word, in private . . .

And right there is the low-water mark of the story.

I've always said that theatre gives you your very best and your very worst moments. I don't think they'll ever again be as extreme or as personal as the ones I experienced during the life of *Blue Sky Boys*.

And they were moments, because as I said, despite our worst fears on that sunny Sunday afternoon, the season was able to play out as planned. Not as triumphantly as envisaged, but people came, the cast worked hard and the audiences responded. It can never be a waste of time or energy – or even money – if that's the case. We're here to play, people come to watch and listen. Outside and underneath slightly ridiculous dreams of glory, fame and wealth, if you're working, if you hang out your shingle and you do your work and there's someone there to bear witness, then the world is in balance.

That's the way I look at things now.

But then I would say that, wouldn't I?

I went back and forth between Wellington and Auckland during the season – getting the box office figures faxed to me daily when I wasn't on-site. My family came up from Rotorua to see the show. I had to admit – as was pretty much apparent during our first week – that I'd lost all my money. Hey-ho.

After our closing night I packed up my stuff from Aunty Ruby's house and drove south. I remember that was the Christmas – there comes one in every parent's life – that we bought the kids a tent. I was running out of cash but there was a TV show I'd be working on in the New Year.

The TV show was canned. It turned into the long dry summer of no work – no TV work, no corporate video work – nothing. Two or three times I got within a week of having to go on the dole. I was the sole breadwinner for my partner and kids. I could never let this happen to me – or them – again.

Interestingly, the rumour went round that I'd mortgaged our house in order to fund the Auckland season, and me and the family were out on the street. Someone in the theatre community had rewritten the story to make it more dramatic. As is their wont.

Some dribbles of TV development work gradually turned into the position of head writer on a new drama series. It went on to dominate my working (and other) life for the next few years, during which theatre had to stop being my focus. Tim came in as a lead character in the second series and Michael had a guest role as well. I somehow wrote a play and got it on at Bats during that time, but it wasn't till much later that I was able to return to theatre in a serious way.

In the years following our run at world-domination-starting-with-Auckland, productions of *Blue Sky Boys* appeared at Court Theatre in Christchurch, Fortune Theatre in Dunedin and Centrepoint in Palmerston North. It also cropped up in Queenstown, being performed by God knows who at the foot of the gondola without notifying me or Playmarket, let alone applying for the rights. Jon Pheloung made it international by staging it at North Carolina State University when he was teaching drama there – thanks Jon!

Most significantly, Tim Balme and Michael Galvin returned to the play with a touring production. By this time they were both *Shortland Street* stars – Tim playing the recurring role of Greg Feeney – and with that show having become an institution with a massive following the time seemed right for them to capitalise on their high profiles.

Simon directed again. I think there was also a sense of unfinished business for all of them. There was more juice in this yet, and it deserved to end on a higher note. They loved the play too, and the demands it made on them. And by now it belonged to them as much as it did to me.

The tour was a success. They played smaller cities – I remember my brother saw them in Tauranga – on a circuit that was just opening up thanks to the growth of regional arts festivals in places such as Taranaki and Taupo. The tour came to Wellington and played Downstage to full audiences. Those were the only performances I saw but I shot a video while they were there. Watching Tim and Michael once more inside the skins of Don and Phil Everly – crooning love songs and spitting venom, ripping out raw rock'n'roll and rollercoasting through hope and despair to finding together one last consolation comeback single – I was happy.

I spent the royalties on a leather lounge suite. Green with stonewash effect. My new partner hated it, and I had to get rid of it when we moved in together.

I didn't go to rehearsals for that touring production, I didn't try to shape the show. It was 'the boys'' go at it – their initiative and their money this time. There was a read-through in the Samoan Church hall across Taranaki Street from the Hope Gibbons building where my office was then (now part of a gym) – I remember that. But nothing more until watching the show at Downstage.

It might just be my imagination now, but when that last version of *Blue Sky Boys* left Wellington it was like a ship sailing over the horizon. It had made a last pass through my life and now I was farewelling it. I felt separate from it – at last. All the hope and excitement and determination and anguish I had poured into it were measured up and found to be equal. It still owed me financially – even with the lounge suite it had cost me more money than it ever repaid – but I couldn't, and wouldn't, put a price on how much it taught me.

Adios amigo.

I didn't get rich. The big house above Scorching Bay is still there, leaves in the pool. Not that I walk by there much, because I live on the other side of town now with someone else. *Blue Sky Boys*, the things and people who gave me the ideas, the places I worked on it and the collaborators I worked with, the milestones that occurred, are all inextricably linked with a time in what is already history, and a phase of my life that is gone.

Maybe that's why I'm sitting here this morning, door open on the blue Mediterranean sky, thinking about the dark-cut shapes of

Wellington, as Katherine Mansfield did ninety years ago standing on the terrace above me. And maybe no one is interested in this sentimental journey but me. Hey-ho.

I haven't talked much about the actual play. And nor am I going to. Reading it back after many years was a pleasant rediscovery. Yes, full of overwritten stage directions and storms of exclamation marks, but intricately and satisfyingly plotted. All the sweat that went into learning my craft paid off I think. Somewhat surprisingly – because I've thought of it as 'early work' for a long time now – it still stands up. For me at least. And its satisfactions lie in the little things that I had forgotten – Pete Fontaine finding his blues harp in the Rockin' Cowboy's guitar case, Don (and us) figuring out it was Carl who alerted Phil to Don's pills – the stitches and tucks by which plot necessity becomes dramatic opportunity, by which questions are answered and motivations elucidated, and the loop closes and the world of the play is complete in itself.

What should be obvious to any reader is that there's nothing 'good-timey' about *Blue Sky Boys*. It's a tough little play, full of anguish and cruelty, owing far more to *Who's Afraid of Virginia Woolf?* than it does to *The Buddy Holly Story*. The tension between harmony and hatefulness is woven through every part of it, there is bittersweet resolution but the ending is much less than triumphant, my infant daughter was right to be disturbed by it. The price of love, indeed.

'Bye Bye Love' always made a fantastic encore after the full-cast curtain call – but in the aftermath of the drama I imagine many an audience member found themselves wondering 'Exactly what is it I'm clapping along to?'

That was always my intention.

Michael and Tim, their performances, guitar playing and singing, came to embody *Blue Sky Boys* not just to the wider public but to me also. In this introduction I've concentrated on that, and on them, but every production was the result of a group effort by talented, hardworking and enthusiastic teams of actors, designers and operators. They also served – with valour and distinction. And good humour.

We drew the bow, the arrow flew . . .

BLUE SKY BOYS – PRODUCTIONS

NZ Playwrights' Workshop, Heretaunga, 1988:

Jed Brophy
Michael McGrath
Melissa Miles
Emma Robinson
Peter McAllum
John (Hone) Kouka
William Walker (director)
Michael Peck (dramaturge)

Bats/St James Theatre, Wellington, 1990:

Tim Balme
Michael Galvin
Emily Perkins
Stephanie Creed
Peter McAllum
Colin Kitchingman
Simon Bennett (director)
Helen Vasbenter (set design)
Gary Henderson (musical director)
Dan Slevin (manager)
Steve Marshall / Simon Rayner (lighting)

Maidment Theatre, Auckland, 1992:

Tim Balme
Michael Galvin
Sassy Acorn
Sue Morrison
Willy de Wit
Darren Young
Simon Bennett (director)
Gary Henderson (musical director)
John Parker (set design)
Steve Marshall (lighting design)
Fenn Gordon (producer)
Simon Elson (production manager)

Touring Production, 1995:

Tim Balme
Michael Galvin
Katie Wolfe
Nicola Murphy
Colin Kitchingman
Peter Hambleton
Simon Bennett (director)
Gary Henderson (associate/musical director)
Phil Blackburn (lighting/sound design/operator)
Simon Rayner (stage manager)
Tait Productions (set design/construction)
Tim Balme & Katie Wolfe (producers)

For Jill

BLUE SKY BOYS

Characters

Don Everly – Pop Star, 27
Phil Everly – Pop Star, 25
Fran – Beatles fan, 16
Jillian – Beatles fan, 16
Carl – Drummer, 16
Pete Fontaine – Radio Personality, 35

ACT 1

Darkness. A drum roll. An announcement – 'Ladies and gentlemen – the Everly Brothers!' Spotlights catch Don and Phil as they leap into 'Wake Up Little Susie'. Polished and professional, they exude excitement, warmth, friendliness and good music, their synchronised movements and voices creating a picture of perfect harmony.

Don: Well if you remember that, I'm sure you'll recollect this one too.

The lights change to a warmer glow. Don and Phil perform a beautifully delicate 'All I Have To Do Is Dream', accompanied by a drummer dimly visible behind them. At the end of the song the lights come up to a more tawdry general yellow. From a free-floating image of their heyday, the Everly Brothers and their performance are now located in a specific place and time – the Buffalo Hall, Wellington, New Zealand in the winter of 1964. It is the end of a disastrous tour and the low point of the Everly Brothers' career.

Don: Thank you. I'd like to welcome you here tonight to the – Buffalo Hall. I'm Don Everly – this is my brother Phil. And – Carl. He's from – where was it Carl? – Hamilton, right here in New Zealand.

We got some more oldies for you tonight, so take the brakes off your wheelchairs and let your hair down. Those of you who've got hair.

Phil strums his guitar, trying to start the next song. Don ignores him.

Just kidding. You're a great audience and we'd love to put you in a Home – I mean we'd love to take you home with us.

Phil, concerned at the way things are going, cuts Don off. Highly unusual as it's Don's accepted role to do the talking on stage.

Phil: Next we'd like to perform our current single. It's a big favourite of ours and I hope it'll soon be one of yours. It's called – 'Ebony Eyes'.

Phil goes straight into the intro for 'Ebony Eyes' to the surprise of both Don and Carl. Carl fumbles, dropping his drumsticks, earning a scorching glance from Phil. Grabbing their opportunity, Fran and Jillian, two young fans, make a dash across the stage. However, rather than flinging themselves at the Everlys, they dodge around them. Jillian is momentarily face to face with Phil before she follows Fran and disappears out the back. Phil plays to the audience.

They told us the girls were fast round here.

He begins the intro again. Don stands apart, as if he's not going to join in the song. However, just in time for his vocal, he does. They perform 'Ebony Eyes'.

Blackout.

The sound of the performance as heard from backstage. The lights come up on the backstage set. A corridor leads down a few steps from the backstage door, past the doorway to the dressing-room, and ends at a closed side-door which opens onto an alley (unseen). On the wall just inside the backstage door is a phone. The dressing-room has a sink-bench, a Zip water-heater, a large stuffed deer head mounted on the wall and various bags, clothes and guitar cases belonging to the Everly Brothers scattered around it. A door from the dressing-room leads into a small washroom with handbasin and a toilet cubicle.

Fran and Jillian burst through the stage door, looking for a means of escape.

Fran: Down here!

They run to the door to the alley. Fran tugs at it desperately but it doesn't move.

Jillian: We'll have to go back!

The music from the other side of the wall ceases. Applause is heard.

Fran: No!

Jillian: But your father's waiting to take us home.

Fran: He's not taking me home! I said we'd see them. I said we'd get their autographs didn't I?

Jillian: I know, but – [how?]

Fran casts round for escape. Jillian hears something.

Someone's coming!

Fran: In here!

Fran drags Jillian into the dressing-room. The stage door opens and Don enters quickly. Fran just has time to pull Jillian into the washroom and close the door before Don is in the dressing-room. He goes straight to his suitcase for something. To his frustration and concern he can't find what he's after. He looks around as if he might have misplaced it or dropped it somewhere. He stops as Phil and Pete Fontaine enter through the stage door.

Pete: Fantastic! Even fans invading the stage, eh?

Phil: Two fans.

Pete: First time that would have happened at the Buffalo Hall.

Phil: We should be up at the Town Hall. That's where we always
              played before.

Pete: That was booked months ago by the Beatles.

Phil: Then why put us on the same night as them?

Pete: I had thought tomorrow. But that clashes with the Annual
              Roar.

Phil: The what?

Pete: The Annual Roar. For the Buffaloes. And the night after that
              is Judo.

              Phil can't quite believe what he's hearing.

Phil: Judo.

Pete: I'm sure things will pick up for the second show. The
              Buffalo Hall came very highly recommended.

Phil: By who?

Pete: Clarrie Thompson.

Phil: He's a promoter?

Pete: Racing commentator.

              And Buffalo.

              Phil places his guitar in its case.

Don: If this is the Buffalo Hall – what's with Bambi?

              He indicates the stuffed deerhead.

Pete: We're a little short on buffalo in New Zealand – I think it's
              the closest they could get. It normally takes pride of place
              in the main hall, but I thought better to move it in here. It's
              a big step for the Buffs – trying out a pop show. I had to
              convince them the place wouldn't be wrecked by hordes of
              Teddy Boys.

Phil turns to Don.

Phil: You see that? He can't even hold his sticks now.

Pete: Young Carl? I was talking to him earlier. Big fan of yours.

Phil: (*to Don*) I thought you were going to spend some time with him?

Pete: Playing alongside his idols. Bound to have a few collywobbles.

Don: (*to Phil*) You wanted him because he was cheap.

Phil hangs up his jacket and strips off his shirt.

Pete: At his age it was all the Blues with me. Mississippi Delta. You'd know all about that. Used to play the harmonica a bit actually.

Don: No! You hear that Phil? We're in the company of a genuine Bluesman!

Pete: Well I wouldn't − [go that far]

Don: What'd they call you − Blind Boy Pete? White Boy Pete?

Phil: Wighead Pete?

Don: Come on − pull out your harp − let's have a jam.

Pete: Well, I . . .

Don: An old twelve-bar sharecroppin' down and dirty blues session.

Pete: That was years ago. I haven't seen my harmonica in −

Don starts an improvised blues song.

Don: Woke up this morning − in the Buffalo Hall

Woke up this morning − in the halfway empty cold and draughty Buffalo Hall

Said you must be Blind Boy Pete − for booking us in here at all!

Pete chooses to see the funny side of this.

Pete: Very good!

Phil: Best song you've written in a year.

Phil heads for the washroom, on a collision course with Fran and Jillian who are hiding on the other side of the door, unable to hear or see very much. Pete remembers the Billboard *magazine in his hand.*

Pete: Suppose you've seen the charts? Couldn't have timed it better with the tour.

Phil stops in the act of opening the door. The girls retreat unseen into the toilet cubicle. Phil lets go of the washroom door, it swings open.

Phil: Timed what?

Pete: You mean no-one's told you? It's the Top Five!

Phil's attention is now well and truly caught.

Phil: Top Five?

Don: Give me that.

Don grabs the Billboard *before Phil can and scans it incredulously.*

Pete: It's a first! Never been done before!

Don starts to laugh. Phil – seized by a wild hope – reaches for the Billboard *but Don keeps it away from him.*

Phil: What? Straight in at Number One?

Don continues to laugh. Phil makes another attempt to see the Billboard *which Don evades.*

Tell me!

Pete: Every single one a Beatles record!

Phil: What?

Pete: In the Top Five! Number One – the Beatles. Number Two – the Beatles. Number Three. Number Four. And at Number Five is the Beatles singing 'She Loves You' –

Don: In German.

Don shows it to Phil – who is flabbergasted.

Phil: That proves it. That proves it. It's like a disease. They're not even singing in English. But it's not English you have to sing in any more is it? It's Limey. It's Scouse.

Don: 'Ebony Eyes' by the Everly Brothers . . .

He scans down the page – turns it over.

. . . Number 73. With a bullet.

Phil: Grown men wearing Beatle wigs, women fighting over cut up bits of their bed sheets – America's gone crazy! Beatle pyjamas, Beatle buttons, Beatle crap from one end of the country to the other!

Pete has realised the Billboard *is not quite the hit he'd hoped for.*

Pete: I'd – better check things out front . . .

He goes. Phil hardly notices.

Phil: It can't last. This whole Beatlemania English Invasion thing is a fad. The next time we see the Beatles we'll be headlining them.

Don: With what? 'Ebony Eyes'?

Phil: 'Ebony Eyes' could still be a hit. It could still do something for us.

Don: I told you I wasn't playing it anymore.

As Phil goes into the washroom –

Phil: They expect it. It's current.

The conversation continues between the two rooms as Phil washes himself at the handbasin. With Phil out of sight Don returns to looking for whatever it is he's lost, anxious to locate it before Phil does. Jillian peeps over the top of the cubicle. Seeing Phil's naked torso she ducks down again.

Don: Current? How current is 73? At least the Beatles are playing rock and roll.

Phil: Rock and roll? They're British for Christ's sake!

Phil tries to sound casual.

We could pull 'Ebony Eyes' if we put in another ballad. Say, 'Prize of Love'.

Don: Forget it.

Phil: I've been working on it, Don. It's ready.

Don: We've been over this –

Phil: I think it could be our next single.

Don: I said forget it.

Phil: (*bitterly*) Maybe you've got a song? Huh? Written anything lately, Don?

Don: And forget 'Ebony Eyes'. If I say we don't play it we don't play it. You pull a stunt like that onstage again and I'll –

A sound stops Don dead. His back is to the washroom. Phil stands in the doorway holding up a pill bottle and rattling it. Don turns.

Phil: You'll what, Don?

Don is stock still for a moment. He steps forward to take the pill bottle but Phil closes his hand.

Two years you cost us.

Don: It's not like before.

Phil: Two years getting you straight. We were never off the charts. Until you messed it up.

Don: Yeah, yeah. Me me me. All my fault.

Phil: You swore.

Don: I can control it, Phil.

Phil: Like you did in England?

Don: They're just to keep me level.

Phil: Level? You've flipped out.

Phil crosses to Don's suitcase and pulls a gun out. An old Colt.45 revolver. He gestures to Don to explain it. Don turns away, caught out.

Are you going to tell me Daddy gave this to you?

Don: I took it. Last time we were home.

Phil: For what?

Don: In case we see any rabbits.

Phil: Where're the bullets?

Don: There are no bullets. I doubt it would even fire now.

He takes it from Phil.

It's just a keepsake. Remember when we'd sneak it out for target practice?

He sights it.

Phil: I'm not likely to forget am I?

Don: You're still on about that. If I'd wanted to shoot you I would have done it.

He aims at Phil, then slightly to one side.

I hit the fence post deliberately.

Phil: You could never hit the fence post when you were aiming at it.

Phil grabs the gun and drops it back into the suitcase.

Don: Yeah – that gun always did pull to the left.

Don holds out his hand for the pills.

C'mon Phil – we've got another show tonight.

Phil: And another show and another show. Down and down, and sicker and sicker . . .

Don: Just give them to me!

Phil: I will.

             One at a time.

Don: (*dangerously*) What?

Phil: This is where things change, Don. You can't look after
             yourself – someone has to do something about getting us
             out of this mess.

             Don laughs disparagingly.

Don: And Fate has appointed baby boy Phil?

Phil: We can get another hit. We can get back up there. If we try.
             That's why you've got to listen – just listen to 'Prize' – give
             it a chance.

             *Phil picks up his guitar and, putting the pill bottle down beside
             him, starts to play and sing 'Prize of Love'. Don paces.*

Don: Yeah – that's . . . that's . . .

             *He makes a sudden grab and, before Phil can stop him, gets the
             pill bottle.*

             . . . just the kind of milky slop that turns my stomach.

             Phil retains his composure.

Phil: I don't think so.

Don: Well, yes I think so. And personally I'd rather jam with
             dickless and his long lost harmonica.

             He toasts Phil with the pill bottle and unscrews the lid.

Phil: Well – nuts to you, Don.

             *Don is dumbfounded to see the 'pills' he has emptied into his hand
             are peanuts.*

             Peanuts in fact.

             Feverishly Don empties the rest of the bottle.

Phil: Don't worry, I've got your uppers. Nice and safe.

Don moves towards Phil's suitcase.

Not in there.

Phil settles himself with his guitar.

You'll get one –

Don: One!

Phil: – as soon as we've played this show. 'Prize of Love'.

Don: You go to hell.

Phil: And 'Ebony Eyes'.

Don throws the pill bottle.

Don: I'm not playing that shit!

Phil: Fine. We'll just sit here instead and watch you kick. That should be a show in itself.

Don seizes on Phil's jacket which is hanging up and goes through the pockets.

I said they were safe.

Enjoying the sense of power, Phil turns out his trouser pockets to demonstrate they're empty. Don fights a rising sense of panic.

Don: They were there before the show. They're here somewhere.

Phil: Get your guitar, Don. If we're putting 'Prize' into the show we'll have to rehearse it.

Don pulls open drawers and cupboards, scattering things angrily in his search. Phil's voice is steely.

If it's not note-perfect, I just might not give you any at all.

Don stops, desperate.

Don: You can't do this to me.

Phil: Get your guitar.

*Don stares at him – then turns and walks quickly out through
the door to the stage. He passes Carl in the doorway without
acknowledging him. Carl stammers.*

Carl: It was those –

But Don is gone. Carl enters the dressing-room.

Phil: Where you been? Signing autographs?

Carl: It was those girls – running across the stage – it put me off.

Phil: A couple of fans?

Carl: Don said we wouldn't be playing 'Ebony Eyes'. He said –

Phil: Of course we're playing it. Why the hell do you think we
            rehearsed it?

*They are interrupted by a repeated crashing sound backstage –
coming closer. Don reappears, flailing the remnants of his guitar
against the wall one last time before entering the dressing room. He
holds the wreckage up.*

Don: Damn thing's gone all out of tune.

He drops it at Phil's feet.

Phil: Excuse us a moment, Carl.

Carl goes back out and waits glumly.

            You think that's solved your problem?

Don: You can lead a horse to crap but you can't make him sing it.

Phil: You know as well as I do what it'll be like – the shakes, the
            sweats, the cramps . . .

Don: I'm your brother!

Phil: Look at yourself, Don. What kind of sight do you think you
            make?

            Maybe you think we've got nowhere to go? Maybe you
            imagine we've come down here to slip off the end of the
            world? It's not going to happen that way, Don. I'm turning

this act around. And I don't care if I have to drag you every inch. Tonight, tomorrow, next week, next year, you're going to be right there beside me – grinding it out for the good people with a smile on your face.

Don slumps into a chair.

There's a million guitars in the world. Guess I'll step out and get you another one.

Phil leaves – heading for backstage. Carl stutters.

Carl: I – [want to go home]

Phil: Not now, Carl.

Phil disappears. Carl turns back, upset. Not wanting to face Don in the dressing-room he pulls at the door to the alley – it won't open – he kicks it and yanks it. It springs open with Pete holding onto the handle on the other side.

Pete: Steady on! Oh – it's you, Carl. Can't be too rough on the place – I've paid a £20 bond to the Buffaloes.

Carl: Sorry.

Pete: I'm just scouting the alley for a couple of stray girls. I've got a Dad out front – on the warpath.

Carl, miserable, doesn't respond.

I envy you, you know Carl. Every day a new town – every night a new audience – the romance of the road, eh?

Carl: I used to dream about seeing them. I'd learn every record until I could play it with my eyes closed and imagine it – the way they put their heads together when they sung.

Pete: They're attractive young men alright.

Carl: And now I'm making a mess of it.

Pete: Of course life on tour can be lonely – I expect you're missing home, family . . . girlfriend . . .

Carl: I don't have a girlfriend.

Pete: Really? I know from first-hand experience how hard it is being separated by the demands of the pop music world. I had a – very close friend. You've probably heard of him – The Rockin' Cowboy.

Carl shakes his head.

He's still a legend in entertainment circles from Kaitaia to Bluff. Though he – passed away – some time ago now. Are you interested in the Blues, Carl?

Of course you are with those sad eyes of yours. You know when I was just about your age some friends who were in the merchant marine introduced me to it. The Blues. They'd bring the records over. Mississippi John Hurt, Howlin' Wolf, Blind Lemon Jefferson . . .

Carl: That's what I wish I was doing – just playing their records, not . . . [seeing what it's really like]

Pete: That settles it. After the show you come up home for a nightcap – and I'll spin you a few discs.

Carl: Well, I . . .

Pete is already going.

Pete: The perfect way to end the evening. Muddy Waters, Robert Johnson – and I've got a Big Bill Broonzy that'll knock your socks off!

He exits to the alley and the door closes behind him. In the dressing-room Don takes the gun out of the suitcase. As he hears Phil coming he quickly sticks it in his belt, hidden by his jacket. Phil re-enters from backstage.

Phil: Seen him?

Don: Blind Boy? Probably out picking cotton.

Phil: He's going have to find us a guitar and fast.

As he turns to leave again, Carl is standing there resolutely.

Carl: I've thought about it –

Phil: You seen him?

Carl: All I'm doing is making you look bad.

Phil: What?

Carl: I thought I could do it – but it was a mistake. Coming.

Phil: Look –

Carl: You don't have to pay me any money. I just –

Phil: Carl –

Carl: I just want to go home!

Phil loses his cool.

Phil: For Christ's sake! You think we're going to stop everything for you? You think I'm going to delay getting out of this piss-ant country for one second because you're feeling sorry for yourself?

Carl looks like a beaten dog. Don has taken a rolled-up pair of socks from his suitcase, and now slips into the washroom, locking the door. Phil changes tack.

Look – Carl – it's a tough call being a pick-up drummer. Having to step straight in, learn a bunch of songs overnight …

Carl: I know the songs. I've got every single one of your records.

Phil: You're probably – over-awed. You keep telling yourself you're not up to it – and sure enough it comes off that way. You think I never felt like that?

Carl: You?

Phil: I spent my whole time as a kid just trying to catch Don up. Practising every day till I had blood under my fingernails. The better I got the more he couldn't stand it. He'd change the song midway to see if he could lose me.

Carl: It's just –

Phil: You know, when I was eight I grew two inches. Just to spite him.

Don tips bullets out of the roll of socks. He methodically stands the bullets up along the handbasin rim.

Carl: It's not like I thought it would be.

Phil looks round the dressing-room.

Phil: Amen to that.

Don loads the bullets into the gun.

You know – Don and me were just talking. We figure as soon as we get back to the States we'll go into the studio to cut 'Prize of Love'. We've got a good feeling about it. We'll probably carry right on and do an album too.

Carl: A new album?

Phil: I won't lie to you, Carl – things have been tough for us. But we're turning the corner. We're going to work our way back. We just need people we can rely on. Starting with a drummer. In the studio, then touring. We're out on the road the most part of the year.

Carl: Me?

Phil: I think you could do it, Carl.

Carl: I could go with you? To America?

Phil: Of course me and Don want to see how you go here first …

Carl: I can play a lot better.

Phil: That's just what I was saying to Don.

Carl: I'll play till I've got blood under my nails!

Phil: Now you're talking.

Don raises the gun to his head and shuts his eyes.

Carl: I knew you wouldn't let the Beatles get ahead of you for long.

Phil: We'll give those rag-mops a run for their money.

What do you say? Forward to Number One?

Don tries to pull the trigger, can't do it, steels himself.

Carl: Top of the Pops!

Phil: Is it a bird, is it a plane? No – streaking in from nowhere, first week in and straight to Number One, it's –

Carl/Phil: THE EVERLY BROTHERS!

Just as Don reaches the point of no return, Jillian peeps over the top of the cubicle, sees Don about to blow his brains out and lets out a piercing scream. All hell breaks loose. Jillian falls down from her perch and she and Fran come tumbling out of the cubicle, becoming hysterical at the sight of Don waving the gun around. They crowd screaming to the door in the confined space, but are unable to get it unlocked and open. Phil and Carl, alarmed, rush to the door but are unable to get in. Every time Don makes a move to help, the girls panic further. Initially startled by Jillian's scream, and now more than a little hysterical himself, Don starts to find the whole thing funny. He begins to mimic the girls' shrieks. Phil, desperate, batters the door with his shoulder and breaks it in. The girls rush out.

Fran: He's crazy!

Jillian: He's got a gun!

Phil enters the washroom and snatches the gun away from Don who is helpless with laughter. Fran pulls Jillian into the corridor. Phil discovers the bullets in the gun.

Don: Phil . . .

Phil hits him hard in the stomach. Don buckles. Phil leans over him.

Phil: I wish you had. At least we might've got a Number One out of it.

Fran and Jillian start toward the stage door but freeze as Pete backs through it, talking to Fran's father who is unseen.

Pete: – Well I'm sorry but I've been into the dressing-room and there are definitely no girls there. They probably missed you in the crowd and caught the bus home.

Hearing Pete, Phil comes out of the washroom, quickly unloads the gun and stashes it in his own suitcase, placing the bullets in his pocket. Meanwhile Pete lets the door close, turns and sees the girls.

Pete: Hoy! What are you doing there?

Fran: Nothing.

Pete: Where did you spring from?

Jillian: Out of the toilet.

Pete: Don't you be cheeky! Backstage is absolutely off-limits. Your father's out there − one of your fathers − wanting to know where you've got to. So scoot. Scoot!

Desperate, Fran suddenly stabs a finger at Carl.

Fran: I'm his girlfriend!

Pete: Girlfriend?

Fran: (*to Carl*) I am, aren't I?

Pete: Carl?

Carl: No!

Pete: No! That sort of brazen behaviour might work on some lads − but Carl has more sense. Now come on − out you go!

Phil goes into charming damage-control mode.

Phil: Hold on there. I think the young ladies have earned themselves an introduction at least.

He extends his hand.

Phil Everly.

Fran: Fran. That's Jillian.

Phil: Well, all I can say is you girls must be big fans.

Fran: Oh, we are! Aren't we, Jillian?

Jillian: We've got every record.

Phil laughs.

Phil: How old are you, honey? Back when we started out you couldn't have been more than a kid.

Jillian glances at a smirking Fran in horror, realising the mistake.

Jillian: Oh no – I mean . . .

Phil: We're just glad to see some girls that don't put us in mind of our grandmothers. Huh, Carl?

After the trouble you've gone to to get in and see us the least we can do is offer you girls a drink.

Pete: A drink?

Phil: Why don't you duck out the front and get us some cokes, Carl?

He guides Carl towards the door.

Pete: But what about the father? He's –

Phil puts his arm around Pete's shoulders and walks him toward the stage door, where a somewhat shell-shocked Carl has already exited.

Phil: You know what it's like for these kids. A few minutes means the world to them.

Pete: I told him they weren't here.

Phil: I knew I could rely on you.

As they go through the door –

Now, we got a little problem with a damaged guitar . . .

Fran squeals with triumph and drags Jillian back into the dressing-room. They come downstage, away from the washroom door, for an intense confab.

Jillian: Fran! He thinks –

Fran: I know! Just pretend you are. I mean, we are.

Jillian: But Fran –

Fran: You want to see them, don't you?

Jillian: Of course! But –

Jillian looks towards the washroom, remembering Don and the gun.

Fran: We won't have to be here for long. You heard him – Dad'll get sick of waiting and think we've taken the bus.

Jillian: You're a real brainbox, Fran – saying you wanted to come here instead.

Fran: Who does he think he is – telling me I can't go?

Jillian: He's sure going to be mad with you.

Fran: I don't care! Have you got your ticket?

Jillian produces it like a holy icon. Fran does likewise. Their suppressed excitement threatens to burst out.

Just another half-hour –

Jillian: And we'll see them.

Fran: John – Paul –

Jillian: George!

Fran: And Ringo!

Fran/Jillian: FAB!!

Their shrieks are like steam escaping from a kettle.

Jillian: Fifteen and a half?

Fran: Ringo's collar-size. Eight?

Jillian: George's shoe-size.

Fran: How big's your house going to be?

Jillian: Huge! A mansion. And I'll have servants.

Fran: So will I. And sometimes me and Ringo will invite you and George over for tea.

Jillian: And afterwards we'll sit around a big fire and play all their records. And dance. And then George and I will get in our

Rolls Royce and drive home. Even though we only live next door.

Fran: And they'll take us with them. All over the world. London, Paris . . .

Jillian: Liverpool!

Fran – do you think you'd . . .

Fran: What?

Jillian: You know. If you got the chance. With Ringo.

Fran: Of course. How else am I going to have his babies?

Jillian: I've made a list.

Fran: List?

Jillian takes out her autograph book. The list is in the back.

Jillian: Of who I'd – you know . . .

Fran reads.

Fran: Prince Charles?

Jillian: I feel a bit sorry for him.

Fran: Ringo's the only man I'll ever let touch me. Ever.

Oh Jillian, wouldn't you just do anything to meet them?

Jillian: And touch them!

Fran: And kiss them!

Phil comes back through the stage door, reassuring Carl who is behind him with cokes.

Phil: He was just fooling around. I told you – it was nothing.

As they enter the dressing-room –

Here you go ladies.

He hands them a coke each, then crosses to his suitcase.

I hope you girls weren't frightened by this little thing?

He holds up the empty gun.

Phil: It's nothing but a toy. I was just telling Carl – Don kept it as a souvenir from a screen test we did for a Hollywood western.

Jillian is impressed.

Jillian: You were in a film in Hollywood?

Phil: Well – they didn't actually make the movie in the end.

Phil returns the gun to his suitcase and, having taken out a half-full bottle of bourbon, locks it.

But you should have seen us in our gun-slinging duds. Me all in white, Don in black. We always did like to play cowboys. I guess Don never grew out of it.

Phil spikes his coke then hides the bourbon inside the bass drum.

So – you girls still in school?

Fran: (*smart*) No. It's night-time.

Jillian: (*confused*) We finish at 3 o'clock over here.

Fran gets up, wanders over to the drumkit and starts to play around on it. Phil picks up his guitar and picks out a tune.

I suppose you've been right round the world?

Phil: My favourite destination.

Carl: I only come from Hamilton.

Jillian gravitates towards Phil. He shows off on the guitar for her.

Jillian: It must be fab – going to all those places. Singing and playing for everyone. I've always thought that must be really hard. Playing the guitar and singing at the same time.

Phil: You learn to master it.

He offers her the guitar.

Why don't you give it a try?

Jillian: (*revelling in the attention*) Oh no!

Phil: If you're any good you can open for us. We could use a support act.

Jillian: I'd die!

Fran: I'll say. You've been stuck on the recorder since Standard 1.

Phil: Come on –

Phil puts the guitar over Jillian's head.

Fran: She doesn't even blow – she just moves her fingers up and down the holes and pretends.

Phil swings his leg over and sits behind Jillian, his hands on her hands, pressing against her. Jillian goes pink with confusion and excitement. Phil positions her fingers.

Phil: Now we can strum – or pick – easy as pie …

He strums the chords to 'All I Have To Do Is Dream' and sings a snatch of the song into her ear. Carl supplies a soft tasteful drumbeat, standing, as Fran still occupies the drum stool. Phil finishes on a delicate arpeggio chord. Fran adds her own inappropriate cymbal crash, to her amusement. Jillian is entranced.

Jillian: Did you write that?

Phil: Well, no, not that one.

Jillian: It's neat.

Phil: Come on, you must have heard it before? It was a big hit.

Fran: Of course, Jillian. It's one of our fave raves. Remember?

Jillian: (*reluctant to lie*) Oh. Yes.

Fran gets up from the drumkit and wanders restlessly around the room.

Phil: Here's one I did write.

He starts to play 'Prize of Love', having to stretch round Jillian to do it.

Phil: It's going to be our next single. Watch my fingers now.

He sings part of 'Prize of Love'. Jillian blushes.

Got it?

Jillian: It's too fast.

Phil: That's a Sunday stroll.

He quickens the tempo of his playing and singing – showing off for Jillian's benefit. As the song changes from 'Ebony Eyes'-style ballad to something pacier, however, a look of realisation comes over Phil's face.

Hey . . .

Excited, he stands, slings the guitar on properly, and continues. Carl sits at the drums and provides a rhythm. Phil enthuses to him.

Doesn't that sound better to you? Like a ballad – but uptempo?

Phil's enthusiasm builds as he plays and sings the first chorus.

That's what it needed all along!

(*to Jillian*) Honey, it looks like you're my lucky charm.

Jillian: It's fab.

Phil: Fab!

Fran: Fab?

Phil: What about – other girls your age. Beatles fans even. You think they'd go for it?

Jillian: Definitely.

Phil: See, that's it. A couple of years off the charts and a whole fresh bunch of kids come up. They just have to find out about us, that's all. All we have to do is get them to listen.

Phil starts playing again, relishing his discovery.

This is nothing, honey – wait till Don's on lead and I take the harmony.

Jillian:	Don't you ever sing just by yourself?

Phil is oblivious.

Phil: People are getting tired of all the 'Howling Haircuts'.

Carl: He had to once.

Phil: They want real music again – with real musicians.

Phil walks away, quietly playing and singing to himself, making sure he's got all the nuances of his new creation. Carl stops playing, eager to tell the story to Jillian.

Carl: It was in England when Don got sick. He had to be rushed to the hospital in an ambulance. Right before the first show of the tour. Phil didn't even know if he was alive or dead. And the whole audience was waiting, more than a thousand people –

Phil: Where'd you get that from, Carl? Some magazine?

Jillian: Isn't it true?

Phil: True enough. Scariest moment of my life stepping out on that stage alone.

Jillian: What happened? What did you say?

Phil: Didn't know if I'd be able to say anything. I just kicked right in. Most of the numbers I sang the harmony line and hoped nobody noticed.

Carl: Tell them about the end.

Carl is stuttering slightly.

Phil: You tell them.

Jillian: What happened? Please!

Phil: Well – I finished my songs – and I took a bow – and . . .

Jillian: What?

Phil: Nothing.

Jillian: Nothing?

Phil: Silence. Complete and utter. It seemed to stretch out so far I figured I'd just start running and not stop till I got back to Kentucky. Then – right out there in the middle of that audience – one guy stood up. And he started to clap. Then all of a sudden everyone was on their feet. It was like a tidal wave or something. Every single one of them stood up and cheered.

Jillian: Fab.

Carl: And they wouldn't stop.

Don opens the washroom door, unnoticed.

Phil: It was the same wherever I went. The whole of England. But that first night – that was something special.

Jillian: What about Don? Was he alright?

Phil: Don who?

Phil laughs.

Don: Well, well –

Phil turns, caught out.

               – company.

Don heads for the bass drum – the standard hiding place – and retrieves the bottle of bourbon. He drinks it through one of the straws that came with the cokes – the only anomaly in his otherwise perfect display of Southern manners. He addresses the girls.

               You'll have to excuse me. I've got out of the habit of finding twenty ladies in my bathroom.

Fran: There was only two of us.

Don: Could have sworn it was more. Didn't it sound like there was twenty of them in there to you, Phil?

Fran: That's Jillian's scream. She's the best screamer in our whole form.

Jillian: Except for Margaret Arnold.

Fran: She's a cheat though. She gets her friends to pinch her.

Phil takes Don aside.

Phil: Don – you were right about 'Prize' – it wasn't ready. But wait till you hear it now. I played it for these kids and they went crazy – they loved it.

Don: That's great, Phil.

Phil: They could be up at the Beatles, but it's us they want to see. They told me kids are already getting sick of the Beatles.

Don: Uh-huh.

Phil: We're on the upswing, I can feel it. We've got time to run through 'Prize' so you can pick it up – then we'll drop it into this show.

Don: Just give me the pills.

Phil hesitates.

Alright – we'll do the song. Just give me them.

Phil: (*almost gently*) I can't trust you, Don. Not after . . . [the scene in the washroom]

Like I said, after the show –

Don: After the show – is just a little bit too far away, Phil.

Phil: We've got a chance here. If we can just hang in – if we don't blow it now – we're going to get it all back. All of it.

I'll help you, Don. We'll do it together. You got off them once – you can do it again. You'll see.

He takes Don's silence for acquiescence.

And –

(*nods towards the bourbon*) – go easy on that, huh?

Stay awake, Carl. Give me five to check things out front – then we'll work up 'Prize' for the show.

On his way out, in his enthusiasm, Phil whirls Jillian around.

Phil: You'll be able to hear it on the radio and tell everyone 'I helped Phil Everly write that!'

Phil exits, leaving Jillian thrilled and breathless. Fran remains unimpressed, single-mindedly focused on the Beatles. Don stands regarding the girls, noisily sucking bourbon through the straw and blowing bubbles. His manner is suddenly more dangerous. He advances on them.

Don: Freshen your drinks?

He takes their bottles and tops them up with a copious amount of bourbon. As he goes to hand them back –

Uh-uh. What's the magic word?

Fran: Please.

Jillian: Please.

Don surrenders the bottles and turns to Carl to top up his.

Don: Carl. Give you a fright back there?

Jillian stops Fran from drinking and hisses.

Jillian: He's been drinking out of the bottle. You might catch something.

Fran: The coke will kill it.

She takes a swig. Don hands Carl his drink.

Don: You – didn't see what he did with my pills?

Carl is uncomfortable.

Carl: Pills?

Don: The ones you saw me take yesterday.

Carl shakes his head.

The ones you mentioned to Phil – right?

Carl: You said they were for headaches.

Don: Got one now you could split wood with.

Jillian: I've got some aspro's.

She produces the aspirin from her bag. Don regards her witheringly.

Don: Good for you.

Don goes to Phil's suitcase. Finding it locked, he roams restlessly round the room looking here and there.

Carl: I'm going to play much better now. Phil said about you taking me –

Don: No Carl – that's what I like about you. Instinctively – instinctively you play the good songs good and the bad songs rotten. You play them stinking awful rotten and I love you for that.

Fran: That gun was real, wasn't it? Your brother said it was a fake one.

Don: I can't imagine baby brother Phil would tell a lie.

(to Jillian) Can you?

Fran: It is though, isn't it? It is a real one.

Don leans toward her confidentially.

Don: Well . . . maybe baby!

He sings a chorus of Buddy Holly's 'Maybe Baby'. Carl picks it up on the drums. Carl goes into the drum break, Don urging him on –

Ra-da-da Ra-da-da Da-dah-da-dah-da-dah

Ra-da-da Ra-da-da Da-dah-da-dah-da-dah!

Don breaks off from the song, talking to Carl.

He got it right. Holly, man. Checked out at his peak. He just went up – and he never came down. Metaphorically speaking.

Carl: *(to the girls)* Don and Phil knew all of them.

Don: Nobody got to him.

Carl: Not just Buddy Holly –

Don: Heaarrrt-beeet . . .

Carl: But Richie Valens –

Don: La-La-La-La-La Bamba!

Carl: The Big Bopper –

Don: HELLOOOOO BAYYYYY-BEH!!

Fran laughs as if it's some kind of joke.

Fran: Those aren't real people.

Don: What?

Fran: You're making it up. Nobody sings like that.

Don: Come on, you must know Buddy Holly? You must have heard of him?

Fran: Buddy Holly?

Don: And the Crickets.

Fran: The crickets?

Jillian: Did they copy their name off the Beatles?

Don stares at her, then turns away.

Carl: Everyone knows Buddy Holly – 'That'll Be The Day', 'Peggy Sue' – if he hadn't have died –

Don: If he hadn't died he'd have ended up like the rest of us. He was lucky. He had the best times.

Jillian: You mean he's – ?

Don mimes a crashing plane. Jillian feels she's put her foot in it.

Sorry.

Don: Two minutes ago you'd never heard of the man and now you're sorry he's dead? No sister, I was sorry.

Sorry I'd been left behind. Sorry there was no-one left to compete with.

Don is drawn back to Phil's locked suitcase.

Carl: Except Phil.

Don: Phil?

Don goes to the drawer by the sink and rummages through it.

You know as a kid he'd do stretching exercises to make himself grow? I'd catch him hanging upside down with weights. That is a bizarre sight. Strange thing is it worked.

He finds a sharp kitchen knife.

He wanted to beat me so bad I couldn't even play a song all the way through without him changing it to something else in the middle.

He returns to Phil's suitcase and tries to pick the lock with the knife as he talks.

There's a story my mother tells about when me and Phil were kids on our Daddy's radio show. Up at five, on-air at six. Different show every day. Seems one night my mama hears something. So she looks into our room. And there I am – singing the whole next morning's programme in my sleep.

And Phil – Phil's harmonising!

Don laughs, encouraging the others to follow his lead. They laugh too.

And it's funny – because – I don't find that funny.

I don't think there's anything – FUNNY – about that at all!

In a burst of fury Don attacks Phil's suitcase, slashing through it with the knife. He reaches inside, feeling for the pills. Frustrated, he pulls out Phil's clothes. The pills aren't there. Jillian and Carl are silenced by this performance but Fran, more than a little drunk, decides the whole thing is hilarious. Don flicks a pair of Phil's underpants at her.

Fran: Yuck!

She flings them away.

Jillian: Fran!

Don clowns, shooting another pair of underpants at the deer's head where they hang on the antlers. Jillian, feeling guilty, picks up the pair Fran has thrown on the floor – as Phil comes through the backstage door, Pete anxiously appearing in the doorway behind him.

Pete: This is New Zealand. There's not all-night music shops on every corner. You don't think a little glue or something . . . ?

Phil regards him witheringly.

I'll keep trying.

Pete disappears. Phil enters the dressing-room and stops short, surveying the scene. Phil looks levelly at Don.

Phil: I told you they weren't in there.

Don: It just exploded, Phil.

(*to girls*) Isn't that right?

Fran: (*laughing*) Just exploded!

Jillian picks up Phil's clothes.

Phil: That's going to cost you an extra hour.

He turns to the business at hand, picking up his guitar and glancing at Carl who picks up his sticks.

OK –

(*to Jillian*) Like I said, honey – wait till you hear the harmony.

Phil plays, with Carl accompanying on drums. Don ignores them.

That's good, Carl. See, Don?

If you've got the tempo – just join in.

Don: Will do, Phil.

Don winks at Carl. Phil begins to sing 'Prize of Love'. Don joins in – in a mocking moronic Okie-type voice, to Fran's amusement. Phil keeps playing grimly.

Phil: That makes it two hours.

              Three hours.

Don: (*still Okie*) Hey girls, wanna see my Surprise of Love?

              He unzips his fly.

Phil: Tomorrow morning!

Don: That story you were telling everyone – the triumphant Phil
              Everly Tour of England? If you were having such a good
              time, Phil – how come you came home early?

              *Fran whispers to Jillian to stay put while she checks the coast is
              clear, then slips out of the room.*

              He didn't tell you that did he, Carl? How he cancelled half
              the dates and couldn't get back Stateside fast enough? Why
              was that, Phil?

              *Fran goes cautiously through the stage door. Phil makes a last
              sincere attempt to entreat Don's cooperation.*

Phil: Just try the song.

              Don seems to surrender.

Don: OK, Phil. I've got it now.

              *Phil starts the chorus. Don goes back to his grotesque Okie send-up.
              Phil can't stand it any more.*

Phil: God damn you!

Don: I'm just doing it like the Blue Sky Boys, Phil.

Phil: You jealous – !

Don: Bet you never heard of them, Carl. When me and Phil were
              kids we'd see the Blue Sky Boys at every county fair, swamp
              meet, wedding or funeral.

Phil: Just because I haven't dried up like you!

Don: Up they'd get. Two old boys. Grey hair blowing round their
              bald heads. No teeth. Just getting up there and howling

along. Never-had-beens – never-would-be's – just too
stupid dumb to know when to give up and go home.

Phil: There's nothing wrong with this song!

He stabs a finger at Jillian.

She loved it!

Don: She'd love it if you sang 'Camptown Races'. Look at her.

Phil: You show some respect!

Don: But that's all you ever cared about, isn't it Phil? Having
enough boppers hanging off you to make you feel like
something.

Phil: Who do you think you are? Everything you've got comes
from them!

Don: They killed it! They killed it with their squealing. Their pin-
up pictures.

Fran returns and motions from the doorway for Jillian to come.

Rock and roll wasn't for kids. It was never meant for
screaming little girls.

Phil: They're our fans! We need them!

Don: Like we needed the rest of them?

Jillian edges apologetically towards the door.

Jillian: Bye.

Phil catches her hand.

Phil: Hey, where're you going?

Don: Promoters, radio, record companies –

Phil: Don't pay him any mind.

Don: – everyone jumping on the bandwagon until the axle broke.

Phil: You can watch the show from the wings.

Don: Dress like this. Play like that. Sing this song. Smile!

Fran: Jillian – come on!

Phil: We'll dedicate you a song this time. How about that?

Don: I'm 27 years old. I'm a grown man. What am I doing singing about high school?

Fran: Jillian!

Don: What happened to my music?

Jillian: (*proffering her autograph book to Phil*) Could I have your autograph?

Don: Autographs?

He snatches the book out of her hands and dances away out of reach, brandishing it. In the hallway the phone begins to ring.

See? That's all we are! We've signed our life away!

He tears a page out of the autograph book. Jillian gasps. Phil lunges at him but trips and falls heavily. Don keeps tearing the autograph book.

Our cheap sold-to-the-lowest-bidder souls!

Fran comes from nowhere to deliver Don a resounding slap in the face.

Fran: You pig!

She snatches the book. Pete enters the hallway. He answers the phone.

We don't want your rotten autographs! We were only hiding here so we could get to the Beatles!

Phil: The Beatles?

Fran: They make you look like rubbish!

Don is delighted.

Don: They're Beatles fans, Phil. They're Beatles fans!

Fran: Don't you laugh. Don't you dare laugh!

Phil: *(to Jillian)* But I played you my song. You said you loved it.

Fran: She loves George and I love Ringo. So there!

Phil: You said it was fab!

Fran: Fab? We just about died laughing when we heard it. Didn't we, Jillian? We just about laughed ourselves sick!

Don snorts. Phil goes white. His voice trembles with rage and humiliation.

Phil: Get out. Get out!

Before they can go, Pete, who has been having an increasingly excited conversation on the phone, bangs the receiver down and bursts into the dressing-room.

Pete: The Beatles! The Beatles!

Everyone stares at him.

The Beatles want to meet you!

Phil: What?

Pete: I spoke to him this minute. John. John Beatle. John –

Fran: Lennon!

Pete: John Lennon!

Fran screams at the mere mention of proximity to her heroes.

You'll never believe it. He said they've written a song. For you. And they want to give it to you! Face to face.

Fran screams even more excitedly.

Fran: The Beatles!

Pete: They haven't penned a dud yet!

Fran: *(to Jillian)* I told you we'd get to meet them! Didn't I?

Highly amused, Don slaps Phil on the shoulder.

Don: Better and better, little brother.

Phil slides out from under his hand.

Pete: Don't worry Carl – we may still have time to fit something in later on.

Phil: You got us a guitar?

Pete: Well – no – but I did find some sellotape.

He produces a roll and stretches out a length of tape. Phil picks up and dangles Don's demolished guitar.

Good lord. You can't go on with that.

Pete realises decisive action is called for.

I've got something at home – it's not quite the same but –

He looks at his watch.

Just time if I put my skates on.

Phil stops him.

Phil: He said it was a new song? They haven't recorded it?

Pete: Written this morning! They're incredible!

Pete dashes out through the alley door. Don is watching Phil closely.

Don: Wait a minute – you're not considering this?

Phil: Just shut up and let me think.

Don: There's nothing to think about!

Fran: What are we waiting for!

Phil turns on her and Jillian.

Phil: What are you still doing here?

Fran: We're coming too. To meet the Beatles! Aren't we, Jillian?

Phil can't believe her temerity.

Phil: You can whistle.

Fran: You have to take us. You've got to!

Phil: I don't have to do a single solitary thing for you.

Fran: But –

Phil: Out!

Fran: We'll tell what we saw! He was going to shoot himself!

Frozen moment.

Jillian: Fran –

Don laughs and claps his hands sardonically.

Don: Seems like blackmail's the popular sport of the evening.

Fran: We'll tell about the gun. We'll tell the police.

Phil: And we'll all say it's just some crazy story – that right, Carl? –
cooked up by some crazy girls who didn't ask nicely enough
for our autographs.

Don: I'll take you.

Fran reacts excitedly.

Phil: What?

Don: Come on, Phil – there's more than just a song here. Why
not squeeze it for every drop?

He drapes his arms over the girls' shoulders and pulls them into him.

(*to Fran*) Huh? Which one's your favourite, honey?

Fran: Ringo.

Don: (*to Jillian*) What about you?

Fran: She likes George.

Don: (*to Jillian*) And what's George like?

Jillian: He's sort of quiet.

Don: Sort of quiet? Ringo's not 'sort of quiet' is he?

Fran: No, he's fab!

Don: Fab! Well, all is not lost. You just play your cards right and
everything could still end up fab for you tonight.

Fran: You mean you will? You'll take us?

Don: Get some music on the radio there, Carl. If we're going to meet the Beatles we've got to get in the mood!

Fran is jubilant.

Phil: Are you nuts?

Don: Let's dance, honey.

Don grabs Fran in a waltz.

Phil: They'll run straight to the Beatles – make us look ridiculous.

Don: Come on Phil – this is what you want isn't it? All the advantages of fame. What difference does it make if it's ours or someone else's?

Phil: Get rid of them. Then we can talk about – [accepting the invitation]

Don: Change partners!

Don lets go of Fran and dances with an uneasy Jillian.

Phil: It wouldn't hurt to at least check it out!

Don: Wasn't this the one who loved your song so much?

Jillian: I did.

Don: When there was something in it for her. Same as all the others.

Phil turns away.

What's the matter, Phil? You didn't actually think it was you they were after? All those girls? So obliging in the bathrooms, on the backseat of the bus, a quick bang behind the backstage curtain? All they wanted was to rub up against the sweet smell of fame. Until finally they rubbed it all off.

Phil: Get them out of here.

Don: (*to Jillian*) You want to see what's behind the coloured lights? I can give you the whole tour – top to bottom. Everly Brothers to motherloving Beatles. Keep your eyes closed and see if you can tell the difference.

He tries to kiss her. Jillian resists, turning her head away.

Don: That's not the way to get yourself to the Beatles, honey. Nothing comes for nothing – everything's got its price.

             After all – I'm the guy who's gonna make your dreams come true. You are grateful for that aren't you?

Fran: Of course we are.

Don: (*still to Jillian*) So why don't we step out in the alley and you can tell me just how grateful?

             Frightened, Jillian breaks away from him.

Jillian: No!

             Don snaps the radio off.

Don: Then forget it.

Fran: Jillian.

Jillian: Let's go now, Fran.

Fran: But Jillian it's the Beatles.

Jillian: Let's go!

Don: Going to the Beatles – going . . . going . . .

             Desperate, Fran plunges.

Fran: I'd be grateful.

Jillian: No Fran!

Fran: Shut up!

Don: Well, well – a volunteer from the audience. See, Phil?

             He grabs Fran by the hair and kisses her roughly.

             She loves me – yeah, yeah, yeah.

Phil: You're sick.

Don: Then get my medicine.

Carl: Give him his pills.

Phil: Keep your nose out. If you want to do something useful then practice.

Carl retreats to his drums and starts to play 'Dream' quietly, singing softly. Jillian approaches Phil.

Jillian: Please. I did like your song. Honest.

Phil turns away in disgust. Jillian goes to Fran.

Fran –

Fran shakes her off.

Fran: Don't you understand? It's the Beatles!

Don: That's right, honey – it's the Beatles. But first it's me.

He gestures towards the alley.

Jillian: Fran I'm scared.

Fran: You're always scared.

She looks at Don. Walks resolutely towards the alley. She gets to the door.

Don: Wait.

She turns.

What's the magic word?

Pause.

Fran: Please.

Don: What can a poor boy do?

He goes out into the alley with Fran. Jillian doesn't know what to do. The intensity of Carl's playing increases, with a rising stinging edge of anger and loss. Jillian looks round wildly.

Jillian: I'm going to get someone. I'm going to get someone!

She turns to run out of the dressing-room. Phil catches her.

Phil: You're not going anywhere.

They struggle.

You saw her. She went of her own accord. She's not going to thank you for dragging anyone else in. Do you want her father to find out? Do you!

Jillian dissolves into tears. Phil lets her go, coming to a decision.

Alright. You want to meet the goddam Beatles –

He grabs his coat and scarf.

– then come on.

Jillian: I can't. Not without Fran.

Phil: Come on!

He turns and marches out – leaving Jillian in tears. Carl's bitter performance of 'Dream' reaches a crescendo. He smashes down on the cymbals. Blackout.

END OF ACT 1

ACT 2

Lights up – the same 'performance' lighting, not located in any particular place or time, as at the beginning of Act 1. Don and Phil perform 'So Sad'. Blackout.

Lights up on dressing-room. It is 15 minutes later. Fran is in the washroom cleaning herself up. Jillian is sobbing on the steps in the corridor. Carl finishes packing his suitcase and heads for the alley with it. He tries to ignore Jillian's distress but can't.

Jillian: She won't let me in. I don't even know if she's alright.

Carl: You shouldn't have pretended to be their fans.

Jillian: I didn't mean to.

Carl: Nothing would have happened otherwise.

Jillian: We weren't even supposed to come here.

Carl: You've still got time for the second show – go to your Beatles.

Jillian: I just want to go home.

Carl: Then go!

Jillian: I can't leave Fran.

She dissolves into a fresh bout of crying. Carl hesitates – then offers his handkerchief. She dries her tears – then blows her nose soundly.

Oh – sorry.

She proffers the handkerchief but Carl indicates she can keep it. Jillian notices Carl's suitcase.

Where are you going? Haven't you got another show?

Carl: I don't care.

Jillian: What about your drums?

Carl: They can keep them. It's all lies. They're just . . . they're just liars!

Jillian can't completely agree with this.

77

Jillian: I thought Phil was nice.

               Carl turns to leave.

               Please don't go.

               He stops.

               I'm worried about Fran.

Carl: What can I do?

Jillian: You're . . .

Carl: What?

Jillian: You're ordinary. That sounds terrible.

               I feel better with you here.

               It's too late to catch a train anyway. And where could you stay?

Carl: I could sleep in the Railway Station. It doesn't worry me, I –

Jillian: I know. You come from Hamilton.

               Carl springs to the defence of his home town –

Carl: That's got – ! [nothing to do with it] There's nothing – ! [wrong with Hamilton]

               He realises from the look on her face Jillian is having him on. They laugh – Carl relaxes – they look at each other shyly.

               You ever been there?

               Jillian shakes her head.

               Don't bother.

Jillian: Do I look all blotchy?

Carl: No.

Jillian: All the girls at school will think I'm stupid. Missing out on a chance to meet the Beatles.

               She looks at Carl.

Jillian: Do you think Fran was right? Do you think I should have said yes?

Carl: I'm glad you didn't.

There's a moment between them . . . interrupted by Pete suddenly entering from the alley.

Pete: The whole town's gone crazy! Everyone says the Beatles were fantastic! The kids screamed so loud you couldn't hear a note!

He throws an arm around Carl, not wanting to be disloyal.

But we'll give them a run for their money, eh?

He is carrying a guitar case covered in travel stickers which he takes into the dressing-room to open. Carl is caught between wanting to leave, attraction to Jillian, and guilt over deserting Pete. Pete pops his head back through the door.

Now you'll be interested in this, Carl. A genuine piece of New Zealand musical history. Come and have a look.

Jillian looks at Carl sympathetically. Carl follows Pete.

The Rockin' Cowboy's guitar.

Pete flicks up the catches but pauses, smoothing his hand over some of the faded stickers and tags which cover the dusty guitar case.

Auckland, New Plymouth, Timaru. Everyone said it was just a matter of time before – Australia.

Pete lifts the lid. Slightly embarrassed, he takes out a crushed, dried-up white rose.

He was very fond of roses.

Fran has started singing 'We Love You Beatles' – quietly at first then louder as it has the desired effect of restoring her courage. Jillian hears this and taps on the washroom door tentatively.

Jillian: Fran?

Pete lifts out the big old semi-acoustic electric guitar and passes it to Carl.

Pete: Feel that Carl.

Jillian: Fran?

Pete sees something else in the bottom of the guitar case. Moved, he picks it up.

Pete: My harp! I must have put it in here after . . .

He blows the blues harp, rustily, a bit emotional.

Carl: It's electric.

Pete: No, no, you just blow in here like this –

Fran stops singing and emerges from the washroom.

Jillian: Are you alright?

Fran walks past Jillian.

Fran: Of course I'm alright. No thanks to you.

Pete: Ridiculous. Thinking I could play the blues.

Fran is self-conscious, nerves taut, full of restless energy. Jillian follows her.

Jillian: What do you mean?

Fran: All that fuss you made. I heard.

Jillian: I was afraid you might get hurt.

Fran: Afraid I might get to the Beatles you mean. Well, you were right. I'm going to meet them. And you're not.

Fran throws herself into a chair. Pete puts the guitar back in its case. He looks at the harmonica again fondly, shaking his head.

Pete: I just wanted to be part of it. I did feel part of it back then.

Phil arrives suddenly at the alley door – as if he's run. He hesitates, upset.

Jillian: I could have gone. I could have gone with Phil. But I stayed because I was worried about you.

Fran: What do you mean? Where's he gone?

Pete: To the Beatles?

Fran: He can't have! Not without me!

Pete: I arranged it all! I assumed – !

As Phil appears in the doorway –

– I assumed you wouldn't be going till after the next show. I thought we'd make up a party!

Fran: Your brother said I'd go – he said he'd take me!

Phil: He says a lot of things.

Fran: He promised! If he doesn't take me I'll scream this place down! I'll tell everyone – !

Phil: He wasn't there! He'll be going later.

The both of us will. It's crazy chaos over there. There wasn't time for anything.

Pete: But you met them? You met the Beatles?

Phil: Sure – a couple of them.

Fran: Which ones?

Phil: They all look the same to me. Hair – accents . . .

Fran: Was it Ringo?

Pete: Could have been Sounds Incorporated – the support act. You could meet them and never know the difference.

Phil: It was the Beatles, right! I met the Beatles! Ringo – yeah it was Ringo.

Fran: Fab!

Phil: He showed me the song he'd written us – and I said I'd bring Don back to look at it.

Jillian: I thought only John and Paul wrote songs.

Fran: Ringo wrote 'Boys'.

Jillian: No he didn't.

Fran: He did!

She starts to noisily sing 'Boys'.

Pete: Of course I get to meet quite a few celebrities. Most of us Disc Jockeys become a bit blase.

Fran: Disc Jockey? I've heard you on the radio. You're on 'Shopping With Dawn' in the mornings. You're always talking about men's trousers and stuff.

Pete: (*to Phil*) I am – between slots at the moment. But it's only temporary.

Fran: My Mum reckons you sound like a real expert on easy-opening fly buttons.

Pete: I'd better – see about opening the doors . . .

Pete exits.

Phil: (*to Jillian*) See? Your friend's fine. There was no need to get in a panic.

Jillian won't look at him

Look – I never did sign that autograph . . .

He has his hand out for Jillian's autograph book but she hugs her bag into herself.

I could give you a guitar pick? Sometimes girls want guitar picks.

I'll buy you a new book – how's that?

Carl: Leave her alone.

Phil: What?

Fran: When are we going?

Phil: Hadn't you better talk to Don about that?

(*to Carl*) Seen him?

Carl shakes his head. Phil is irked by the unspoken reproach he feels from Jillian.

If I hadn't stopped you no-one'd be going to meet the Beatles. Especially not the two of you.

Fran: No! He said me. Just me!

Phil: Well I'm saying she comes too.

Fran: All she did was try to ruin it! She doesn't deserve to meet the Beatles!

Jillian: I don't want to go anyway.

Fran: Good! The Beatles only want to meet real fans.

Jillian: I am a real fan.

Fran: You liar! You wouldn't even do one thing for George! Or any of them!

Carl: At least she's not a . . . [slut]

Fran rounds on him.

Fran: What? Not a what?

Jillian: She is not!

Fran snatches up the drumsticks.

Fran: Rat-a-tat-tat! Drummer boy! That's all you are!

Carl: Then what's Ringo?

Phil: Leave the equipment alone!

Carl cuffs the drums disparagingly.

Carl: It's all junk anyway.

Phil: What's the matter with you?

Jillian: Everything's spoilt. And your father's going to be really mad. Please Fran –

Fran starts to sing 'We Love You Beatles' again, over Jillian's remonstrations. And keeps it up.

Carl crosses to Jillian.

Carl: Come on – I'll take you home.

Phil: Where the hell do you think you're going?

(*to Fran*) And you – shut up!

Fran doesn't.

I said – !

Fran: Oh, Beatles . . .

Don's voice joining in is heard from out in the alley. He enters, waving the nearly empty bottle of bourbon to finish the song solo.

Don: Beatles we love yoooou!

He surveys the scene, everyone frozen.

I see the party's already started.

Phil: Where did you get to?

Don: Back to the hotel.

Phil regards Don's dishevelled appearance.

Phil: To freshen up?

Don: You know, our room is so messy. Stuff spread all over the floor. Mainly your stuff as a matter of fact.

Phil: I could have told you your pills weren't there either.

Fran: When are we going to go?

Don: Go where?

Fran: To the Beatles! He's been!

Don looks at Phil.

Don: The Beatles. Yeah – I passed the Town Hall. Some crowd. Traffic stopped. Women having babies. Strange signs in the Heavens.

Phil: We need to talk.

Don: I heard tell a row of cops got torn to ribbons by all those little girls.

Phil gestures towards the washroom.

Phil: In here.

Don: Yes sir, apparently there wasn't a dry seat in the house.

Pete comes back.

Pete: Whoops! In all the excitement I forgot to show you the guitar.

Phil: I'm sure it's fine –

Pete's already lifting the lid of the guitar case.

Pete: I don't know much about these things myself –

Don reacts with interest.

Don: Gibson Archtop. Full body.

Pete: It's been under my bed that long I'd almost forgotten it. I hope it's alright.

Don: Are you kidding? They could have buried one of these in the pyramids and all you'd have to do is shake the sand out and plug it in.

Having lifted it out of the case he is examining it with real pleasure.

You play this?

Pete: It belonged to a friend. He died in a car crash.

Don: On the road?

Pete nods.

Pete: Ran into a cow.

Don: You don't say.

              Pete is a bit emotional.

Pete: Excuse me –

              He goes out again. Phil – less than impressed – takes the guitar from Don.

Phil: Forget about that – we'll play with one guitar. Right now we've got some plans to make.

              He guides Don into the washroom.

Don: Hey, you can't be taking me in the washroom, Phil. I'm your brother!

              Phil pushes the door to.

Phil: You finished now? You've made your point?

Don: Depends on what yours is. You saw them?

Phil: While you were – otherwise engaged.

Don: And?

Phil: You saw it from the outside – people going bananas. It's a cross between the Alamo and Grand Central Station over there. Too noisy to do anything but say hello. But – seeing those fans going apeshit – it decided me. We take this song – whatever it is.

Don: I don't believe you.

Phil: If they can chart singing in a foreign language then anything with their name attached has got to go gold.

Don: You hate the Beatles.

Phil: We can tour till we're cross-eyed for all the good it'll do us. We need a single. We need a hit.

Don: Listen Phil – I don't mind going over there to party. To drink with John, Paul – Jesus and Judas. I don't even mind drinking to them. Huh? Salute the coming of their age – and the passing of ours. But there's no way I'm going begging for any song.

Phil: It doesn't matter if it's 'Doggy in the Window'. As long as we get it out before their five minutes in the big time expires – it's a guaranteed Number One.

Don: Not our Number One!

Phil scoffs.

Phil: You're not going to stand on your dignity now?

Don: I'm still Don Everly.

Phil: Don Everly could write.

Don't you understand? This could be our last chance!

Don: Don't you understand? We've had our last chance. It's over!

It's over, Phil.

Phil: No.

Don: Yes.

Don has at last said it.

We drew the bow. The arrow flew. Now let's drink to gravity. And have the – grace – to get out of the line of fire. Before the Beatles – or all the other Beatles to come – turn our asses into pin-cushions.

He turns to leave. Phil puts out his arm to stop him.

Phil: Where do you think you're going?

Don shrugs his hand off.

Don: Home.

Phil: That's a long flight to make – in withdrawal. By the time you get to L.A. they'll have to pour you off the plane.

Don stares at him, then turns to the door again.

I'm grabbing hold of this, Don. With or without you. You might have burnt out. But you're not going to drag me down with you.

Don: Drag you down? You've been hanging on my coat-tails since the day you were born.

Phil: The only thing on your coat-tails is your own sorry behind.

Don: You think you're ready for me? Huh, Phil? You think you're finally ready for me?

Phil: I've been ready for you for years.

Don expresses disbelief.

'When Will I Be Loved?'

Don dismisses this disgustedly, he's heard it so many times.

'When Will I Be Loved?'! You knew when I wrote that it'd be a hit. That's why you wouldn't let it out as a single!

Don: The same old crap.

Phil: You couldn't stand to see me get better than you. You had to keep your foot on my neck. But no more. I'll get that song for myself. Solo.

Don laughs.

Don: Solo? You forgotten England already, boy?

Phil: If it wasn't for the family I would have dumped you then, the first time you tried to – !

Don: The first time I tried to kill myself.

Phil: You couldn't even do that properly.

Don: OK Phil – you think you've got something to prove? Then prove it – out there.

Phil: I'm not playing that game with you. Don – !

Don storms out of the washroom, picks up Phil's guitar and tears the playlist off the back of it.

Don: No playlist. No limits.

He tosses the guitar to Phil.

Phil: As rehearsed. We do it as rehearsed!

Don: Just you and me, Phil.

Phil: You may want to make an idiot of yourself – !

Don picks up the electric guitar.

Don: You and me.

Pete bounces in from the stage door.

Pete: Full house! Every seat's full!

Don and Phil's gazes are still locked. Pete doesn't notice in his excitement.

Didn't I tell you, Carl? This show's going to be –

Phil: Cancelled.

Pete: What?

Phil: The show's off.

Phil places his guitar back in its case.

Pete: You're joking.

Don: You chickenshit –

Phil: I asked for a guitar – not some antique!

Pete: But it's capacity!

Don: It's not the guitar is it, Phil?

Phil: And look at him! He can hardly stand up! I'm not going on with him like that.

Don: Drunk or sober – standing up or laying down – I could play you off the stage any night of the week.

Phil: I'm not playing that game any more.

Don: You know it and you're scared to let anyone see.

Pete: Please. You've got to perform. The Everly Brothers Fan Club from Upper Hutt arrived in a bus!

Phil: Last chance, Don.

               Don makes chicken noises at Phil. Pete scrabbles in his wallet for money.

Pete: Look I'll give you another ten pounds. Out of my own pocket.

Phil: You come with me across there now or we're finished.

               Pete appeals to Carl.

Pete: You tell him, Carl. Tell him.

               Carl's bottled-up anger and frustration at Don and Phil abruptly bursts forth.

Carl: You make me sick! I wish I'd never met you!

Pete: Carl! That's not very helpful!

Carl: I could keep on believing it! Like you made everyone believe it. The way you put your heads together to sing, it was like …

Jillian: Like swans.

Carl: But it's all fake. You're nothing but fakes!

Phil: Yeah? Well I've seen wind-up monkeys that were better drummers.

               Carl attacks Phil, throwing a wild punch. Phil is forced to duck underneath it and hit Carl hard in the solar plexus. Carl collapses. Pete cuts across the melee.

Pete: Alright!

               Fifteen pounds.

               Silence. Don hefts the electric guitar.

Don: I'd better see if this thing'll tune.

               Phil scoffs.

Pete: You'll play?

Don: I'll play so they forget there ever was a brother.

Pete exits to the stage, Don turns to follow.

Phil: That'll be the day-ay-ay -

Don: That you die.

Don heads for the stage. Phil hesitates, in a quandary.

Carl: He's right, isn't he? That's what he meant about that tour of England. You're too scared to go solo.

Phil flexes his sore hand and looks at Carl.

Phil: You know what's really funny? You actually believed we'd want to take you back to the States.

Blackout.

Expectant audience noise. Lights up on performance area. Pete takes the microphone.

Pete: Ladies and gentlemen – in a last-minute alteration to tonight's programme – a special world premiere – for the first time on any stage . . .

He is interrupted by a blistering wall-of-sound guitar intro from Don (cf. the Beatles' 'Revolution'). Don pushes Pete aside and dives into 'Blue Suede Shoes', playing as if his life depended on it. It's raw and energised. Suddenly Phil dashes on with his guitar and muscles in. Don changes the song. Phil changes it to something else. Phil and Don vie back and forth, trying to anticipate each other's next move across 'Blue Suede Shoes', 'Long Tall Sally' and 'Claudette', their rivalries and tensions reaching a peak and being expressed directly through their music. Abruptly they are cut off by a thunderous drum intro as Carl suddenly appears, drumming for everything he is worth. Stunned for a moment, Don and Phil quickly pick up the song 'Temptation'. The combatant strands combine to produce high octane rock'n'roll in a thrilling performance. At the end of the song Carl drives them on once more. Don picks up the guitar intro and announces – 'This is by my baby brother Phil' – before roaring into 'When Will I Be Loved?' and a triumphant finish. Blackout.

Lights up on Fran and Jillian. Music (the performance we've just seen) can be heard through the wall. Fran is at the basin in the washroom. She moves one of the socks Don has left there and something falls from it – rattling into the handbasin. Fran picks it up – it is an extra bullet. In the dressing-room Jillian looks dolefully at her Beatles ticket.

Jillian: I suppose they're on right now.

She crumples the ticket and drops it on the floor – but then sighs, picks it up again and smoothes it out. Fran has quietly crossed to Phil's suitcase and taken the gun out. She examines it, then creeps up behind Jillian and jabs it at her.

Fran: Bang!

She laughs at Jillian's startled reaction.

I knew it was a real one.

She shows Jillian the bullet.

See?

Jillian: Fran, that's dangerous!

Fran traces round her lips with the bullet like a lipstick.

Fran: Don't be such a scaredy-cat.

Enjoying the effect on Jillian, she toys with pushing the bullet into the chamber of the gun. At a certain point the bullet goes in and stays in.

Jillian: Why did you do it, Fran?

Fran shrugs it off.

Fran: Nothing happened.

Jillian: But it did.

Fran: Nothing happened!

Jillian: I thought we'd have fun tonight. I wish the Beatles had never come here now.

Fran: Don't you dare say that!

Jillian: I just want to wake up tomorrow and –

Fran: Don't talk about tomorrow! I don't want to think about it!

Jillian: What's the matter with you, Fran?

Fran: Nothing ever happens here! The Beatles are the first thing
ever to happen! And then they'll just be gone again!

              Don't you see, Jillian? After tonight, they'll just be gone.

Jillian: They're only a pop group.

Fran: No.

Jillian: That's all they are.

Fran: No, Jillian!

Jillian: Just a pop group!

Fran: NO!

              *Fran wildly points the gun at Jillian. The door to the stage flies
              open. Don and Phil enter, exhilarated.*

Don: They were climbing the walls! Did you see that?

              Pete appears behind them in the doorway.

Pete: Terrific show! Terrific!

              *Fran drops the now-loaded gun back into Phil's suitcase as the
              Everlys enter the dressing-room.*

Phil: You see, Don? We can still do it!

Don: Rock'n'roll – that's what we are!

Fran: I'm ready to go to the Beatles now.

Don: Babe, you're looking at the best damn rock'n'roll group in
the world!

              *Carl enters behind them, clapped on the back by Pete as he passes.
              Pete lets the door swing shut and disappears.*

Phil: With Carl the Man on drums! See him go, Don?

Carl ignores him and crosses the room to pick up his suitcase.

It was like the Opry again.

Don: The Grand Ole Opry!

Phil: Two funny looking kids. They laughed when they saw us.

Don: Until they heard us.

Phil: No-one had heard that sound before.

Don: 'Bye Bye Love'.

Phil: And 'Bye Bye Love'.

Don: And 'Bye Bye Love'! Three times before they'd let us off the stage.

Phil: See, Don? That was a hit because it was new.

Don: And because we fit it. It was us – our time.

Phil: Like the Beatles are new now.

Don: That's where we belonged.

Phil is hardly listening, shrugging himself into his coat.

Phil: Come on – get your coat on.

Fran: I'm ready!

Phil: You won't believe the cop on the door over there. He says to me –

Don: Whoa – Phil – what are you talking about?

Phil: If he gives us any crap this time –

Don: Phil. We don't need the Beatles. We just proved that.

Phil: We proved we've still got the fire. All we've got to do –

Don: Is go back to what we were. Little Richard songs –

Phil: What?

Don: Bo Diddley – Gene Vincent – Jerry Lee . . .

Phil is dismayed.

Phil: You think anyone wants to hear that stuff anymore?

Don: We were great out there. You heard them.

Phil: That's fine for some cornball place so far out in the sticks they've just found out the War's ended.

Don: You loved it.

Phil: People want new sounds now.

Don: I loved it.

Phil: That's not going to get us on the charts!

They stare at each other uncomprehendingly as their common ground once more yawns into a gulf between them.

Please Don ... please come with me.

Don: We'd lose everything.

Phil: What've we got to lose that we haven't lost already?

I'm begging you, Don. I'm begging you as your brother.

Don turns away.

I'll tell you where the pills are.

Don looks back at him.

When we get back you can have them. All of them.

Don is fighting – shaking his head.

Don: No Phil.

Phil: Then you can rot. And I'll get that song for myself.

Don: Let's talk. We've gotta talk, Phil –

Phil: They'll give it to me. I saw them – I saw all of them! They're fans. You would have thought I was their long-lost cousin the way they got round me –

Don: (*desperately*) Let's – play. We can come up with something.

Phil: They said if their song couldn't be a hit for the Everly Brothers then the next best thing was Phil Everly's first Number One. But I wanted to give you a chance.

Phil picks up his suitcase, Fran grabs his arm urgently.

Fran: I'm going too!

Phil shrugs her off.

Don: Phil. Phil, don't go back there.

Fran turns back to Don.

Fran: You're going. You said you'd take me. You promised.

Don: Your song – 'Prize of Love'. We'll do something with that.

Fran flings herself at Don.

Fran: You promised! You promised to take me to the Beatles!

Don screams at her.

Don: Get away from me! Can't you see I'm sick!

You can't walk out on me, Phil.

Phil stares at him for a moment – then turns to the door.

No!

Don turns and is confronted by Fran, totally wired, pointing the gun at him.

Fran: You said you'd take me. And you're going to. Now.

Everyone freezes. Jillian is horrified.

Jillian: Fran!

Don slowly advances towards Fran.

Fran: I'll kill you. I will.

Don: That won't work like that, honey. You need to pull the hammer back.

He reaches over slowly and cocks the gun.

Don: See? Now it'll fire.

Fran's voice trembles.

Fran: You take me.

Don continues to move closer.

You – promised . . . To Ringo.

Don: Ringo's a big star. He doesn't need my second-hand leavings.

His chest hard up against the barrel of the gun, Don keeps moving forward, forcing Fran back step by step.

You think you're special? You'd just be one more piece of meat to him.

Fran's breath is coming in gasps.

Fran: No . . .

Don: Not even fresh meat. You think he'd look at you now? You think he'd touch you with a pole now you're stale – secondhand – used-up – stinking of everyone you had to screw just to get to him – ?

Fran: NO!

Both Jillian and Carl start forward.

Phil: Leave him.

Phil walks up to Don.

Getting little girls to do your work for you now?

He takes the gun off Fran. She slides down the wall with a destroyed wail.

You've always been weak. I just couldn't see it. I always thought you were so great. Was so proud when we were kids just to be standing alongside you.

He shakes his head.

Phil: Well, if you want to kill yourself so much –

Phil pushes the gun into Don's hand and raises it to Don's head.

– go ahead.

He steps back, leaving Don holding the gun to his head.

Go ahead and do it. Do it!

Jillian: (*held by Carl, her confidence in Phil's handling of the situation rapidly ebbing*) No, no.

Don sags.

Don: I can't. I can't do it, Phil.

With the release of tension Jillian rushes to Fran. Phil takes the gun off Don.

Phil: Of course you can't.

He shows Don the bullets from his pocket.

I've got the bullets. See?

He places the gun under his own jaw and pulls the trigger.

It's empty.

He points the gun at Don and pulls the trigger again.

As empty as you.

Jillian, who has been preoccupied with Fran, suddenly realises what Phil is doing.

Jillian: NO!

She breaks away from Fran and knocks Phil's arm up just as he pulls the trigger a third time. The gun goes off, hitting an antler of the stuffed deer head. The antler collapses. Everyone is stunned, realising how close they have come to tragedy. Phil and Don stand staring at each other. Don exhales.

Phil: You – !

He lunges at Don, grabbing him by his shirtfront – but his strength ebbs away.

You were meant to take care of me.

Jillian: I saved him. Did you see me, Fran? It was me. I saved him!

Fran sobs. Phil seems to collapse.

Phil: You're the oldest. You were supposed to take care of me.

(*crying*) If you'd just said one thing – one thing I'd ever done – well.

We see Phil for what he is – 25 years old, carrying the weight of the world. Don reaches out to him.

Don: Phil.

Phil shakes him off. He staggers away, collecting himself.

Tell the Beatles –

Phil: There were no Beatles. There isn't any song. I didn't even get past the cop on the door.

Jillian: But – you said you met them.

Phil: Our names weren't on his list. He said 'Everly Brothers – no-one's tried that one yet'. People were laughing. Pushing up behind me. 'Where's your brother then? Where's your brother?' And this cop – this fat cop – says 'Sing something. If you're a pop star – sing us one of your hits.'

And I couldn't. I just stood there – humiliated. Because I'm the harmony. I sing the harmony line.

Jillian: On the phone – the message from John ...

Phil: Just like that time in England. All that applause – out of pity. Because they felt sorry for me – all alone up there – without my brother.

Jillian: It must have been someone pretending.

Fran: A joke. It was someone playing a joke.

She laughs brokenly, then – turning the remains of her spite particularly on Phil –

Fran: Well the joke's on you. Because you're nothing. Nothing! No-one will even remember you!

Don: That's enough.

Fran: (*whimpers*) Don't you touch me.

She backs towards the door.

Don: Seems like you had yourself a date with the Everly Brothers. You usually have to win a competition for that. Things could have been worse. You could have met Ringo.

Fran collapses on the steps sobbing. Jillian goes to follow her but hesitates, looking at Phil sitting slumped and beaten. She takes out her tattered autograph book and approaches him.

Jillian: Could I have your autograph?

Phil looks up at her for a moment. He signs.

Goodbye Phil.

Phil: Goodbye . . .

Jillian: Jillian.

Impulsively she kisses him. Holds it. It is what she will most remember from this night.

She goes out to Fran, speaking gently.

It's late, Fran. We have to go home.

Fran: I only wanted to see Ringo.

Jillian: I know.

Fran: I only wanted to meet him. And I didn't even see them play.

Jillian: They'll come back, Fran. You'll see. And we'll meet them. Just like you said. Everything will be just like you said.

Jillian takes Fran out through the alley door. They disappear.

Pause.

Don: Some night, huh?

He strums the Rockin' Cowboy's guitar.

Give me a rhythm here, Carl.

Carl starts purposefully after Jillian and Fran.

Come on, Carl – we got work to do.

Carl: Work?

Don: A song to write.

Carl: What's wrong with you? Why can't you . . . ?

Don: Be like you imagined me? Like you imagined us? You've gotta make up your mind. Whether you're a musician or just another fan.

Carl: I'm leaving.

Don: Why?

Carl: Why!

Don: Because I did this, and Phil said that? Because we didn't turn out how you wanted us to be? What does it matter? What does any of it matter? Only the music counts.

Carl: Your music is a lie.

Don: What was your best moment today? Huh? It was out there, wasn't it? Playing, performing, feeling it running out of your fingers into the air. You don't stutter when you play. That's what makes you like me.

Carl: I'm not like you.

Don: Then get out – and let me play my guitar. Let me write my song. Let me do the one thing that I can do – that I just happen to believe I was set here on this planet to do. To take the sweaty shirts and the shitty food, the late nights and the cat piss dressing-rooms – to take my whole life, the whole goddam universe – and squeeze it down into a little two-minute song about a boy and a girl.

Because it just seems to me – that's a worthwhile thing to do.

Don turns back to the guitar. As Carl wavers, Pete enters from the stage in high spirits humming 'She Loves You'.

Pete: That's it! All locked up! Now it's B-B-B-Beatles time!

Using one of the mirrors Pete combs his hair straight down into an absurd Beatle mop-top.

What do you reckon? John, Paul, George, Ringo – and Pete!

(*shakes his mop-top*) Woooo!!

Pete becomes aware of the rather down mood – Phil still sitting dazed and exhausted, Don absorbed in putting together chords on the guitar, Carl hovering awkwardly outside the dressing-room door.

We – popping straight over are we? Don't want to leave it too long – or they'll be gone. 'Elvis has left the building!'

No response. Pete recognises the signs only too well.

Don't tell me. It's off. You're not going. Or you've already been – or they popped across while I wasn't looking – or God heard something interesting was about to happen to Pete Fontaine and struck all four of them with a bolt of lightning!

He rallies slightly.

On the other hand – back to Plan A, Carl? Round home for that nightcap?

Carl doesn't meet his eye. Pete takes in Carl's suitcase.

Oh. I see. Fine. I probably need an early night anyway. I lead such an exciting life.

To cover his disappointment –

I'll just shift His Grand High Stuffedness back to pride of place and – [be off]

He sees the disfigured deer head.

Pete: Oh no. That's it. I'll lose my bond! I might as well kiss the Buffaloes goodbye. They'll never let me have a show in here again. Unless I could . . .

He wrestles the deer head off the wall and manoeuvres it through the doorway.

I've got some Uhu at home – that might hold it . . .

Out in the hallway he bumps into something and a shower of pills cascades out of the mouth of the deer head, scattering over the floor.

Oh my God it's the teeth.

Carl steps into the breach.

Carl: They're Don's. He gets headaches.

Carl starts to gather the pills up. Pete is confused as to what Don's headache tablets are doing in a stuffed deer head, but is beyond caring. He wrestles the deer head towards the stage door.

Pete: If I could just fit it in a taxi?

More pills fall out. Pete stops to pick them up. Carl has entered the dressing-room and now holds out his cupped handful of pills to Don. Don looks at him, takes one pill, then closes Carl's hands around the remainder.

Don: Why don't you hold onto the rest for me, Carl?

In the hallway Pete picks up the deer head by its 'good' antler. It comes off in his hand. The head falls on his foot.

Pete: Bugger!

Exasperated, Pete vents his frustration and disappointment by giving the deer head a good kicking.

Bugger, bugger, bugger!

He looks at the pills in his hand.

Pete: Headaches. Tell me about it.

He swallows the handful of pills, then exits through the stage door, leaving the deer head where it lies. Don continues building up a song on the electric guitar – welding the chords into a driving raw-edged rhythm which Carl picks up on the drums. Phil ignores them. He gathers up his guitar and suitcase and walks out of the dressing-room and – as Don sings – out the alley door. Don keeps singing. The lyrics are those of 'Prize of Love'. Phil reappears – listens – then re-enters.

Phil: You can't use my lyrics. With that.

Don addresses Carl.

Don: Might put some kind of spin on. Maybe – 'The Price of Love'? Huh?

Phil hesitates. Don continues playing, feeling his way through the song, talking as if to himself, pulling a face as he takes a wrong turn.

Where'm I going here? E7 – into a chorus of A7 – to B7 – into . . .

Phil: D7.

Don appears doubtful.

Don: D7?

Phil: Sure.

He takes out his guitar, props his knee up and demonstrates. Don echoes it on the electric. Finding it satisfactory, he incorporates the chord change as he plays the song through, Carl accompanying. Phil straps on his guitar and joins in. The Everly Brothers will see another day. Don stops short at a particular point.

Don: Needs something. To give it a feel. Fill it out.

Carl: Drum solo.

He does one. They start to fool around.

Phil: Banjo breakdown.

Don: Blue Sky Boys gee-tar.

He does some hillbilly picking. A strange sound is heard. Pete enters from the stage door, high, playing his harmonica for all he is worth. He leaps clear over the still recumbent deer head. Seeing the others watching he breaks off.

Pete: Sorry. Too loud? I don't care!

He laughs hysterically.

I don't care if I am too loud! I don't care if I do look ridiculous!

He tears his wig off and flings it in the air.

The place is wrecked. The Beatles are off! And I feel like bloody well playing the Blues!

Don: Alright! Let's jam.

Pete: Eh?

Phil: Worth a try.

Don: When I nod my head – give us a blast.

Pete can't believe it.

Pete: You want me? You really want me?

Don: You ok, Carl?

Carl nods.

Phil?

Don hesitates beside him for a moment.

You know, one thing about those Blue Sky Boys. They sure did love to play didn't they?

Pete: This is terrific! Me – jamming with the Everly Brothers!

Don: OK band – 1, 2, 3, 4 . . .

They play the embryonic 'Price of Love', Don signalling Pete's harmonica fills. The playing is loose but full of the drive and excitement of the new. The lights slowly fade. Suddenly the performance lights spring up and Phil and Don step into a full-scale, polished and triumphant performance of 'The Price of Love'. This performance is looser, more dynamic than the opening bracket but still choreographed to accentuate the highlights in the music – e.g. simultaneously 'hitting' the mic to sing, then splitting away at the same moment. Following this they perform 'Cathy's Clown'. At the end they bow. Blackout. Curtain call.

ENCORE

Don: Phil and I would just like to say – bye bye . . .

They perform 'Bye Bye Love' in classic style – acoustic guitars, no drums.

THE END

JOHN, I'M ONLY DANCING

INTRODUCTION

What can I tell you about this one? That this is its first outing in any form. At time of publication it has yet to be produced, despite being written getting on for twenty years ago. Only a handful of people have even read it. I've sometimes referred to it as my 'great lost play' – so it's satisfying that it gets to take a bow on some sort of public platform here, even if it's not exactly the 'boards' that would really bring it to life.

The stock answer to why *John, I'm Only Dancing* hasn't been produced is that the music rights to David Bowie's *Ziggy Stardust* songs are too difficult to obtain or not available. There is of course truth to this. The play was written at a time when – subsequent to the first production of *Blue Sky Boys* – it seemed that you could get any song, and cheap too. The Iron Curtain and New Austerity that soon fell across the world of using-music-in-plays rapidly put a stop to that. At one point we had an agreement in principle with EMI Australia (I think) which was never tested by an actual production – and presumably fell by the wayside. In more recent years Bowie himself has mentioned his interest in adapting *Ziggy Stardust* into a musical, which (again theoretically) would not predispose him to licensing the music to other shows.

But the truth is no-one so far has passionately wanted to put the play on enough to actually find out. In applying for rights it's necessary to be able to say what you're doing and when and where you intend to do it, and nobody's got to that point. On the other hand, as already mentioned, hardly anyone's read it. Why not, I wonder? Why haven't I pushed it harder?

One reason is perhaps the fact that it's a very challenging play to produce. Starting with the casting – seven actors (out of eight) who can sing and dance (six of whom can convincingly play seventeen-year-olds, and one of them able to play guitar like Spiders guitarist Mick Ronson) and perform forty minutes of full-on music while jumping in and out of some fairly intense dramatic scenes. In New Zealand terms it's a big production – at least a three-piece band in addition to the eight actors. So the size of theatre or venue that would make that potentially economic becomes a factor – and it's difficult to imagine any of the established theatres in New Zealand taking a punt on *John*.

Because of course it's not the musical that Bowie has perhaps been musing on – it's a notional school production with rather squalid scenes of school life sandwiched between. If the Bowie music represents the sacred in this equation, then the profane is liberally provided by the body-function-oriented, callous gallows humour and grim and desperate hand-to-hand fighting which typified a New Zealand boys' high school in the mid-seventies – more like a war at times than an education. Like the other plays in this volume, *John, I'm Only Dancing* is not an easy watch. But out of the sour and sweet, the rough reality and the smooth gleam of Glam, could/should come something alchemical which fuses those two seemingly light-years-distant worlds.

One other reason *John* might have got left behind on the starting blocks is that it was the second of two plays I wrote in the same time period. In 1992 I applied to the Queen Elizabeth II Arts Council and was awarded the QEII Writers Bursary. This was a huge break for me, rescuing me from financial anxiety and allowing me to write uninterrupted for six months. In my application I had pitched as my project *The Temptations Of St. Max*, but I knew that with the time and money I could write more than that. I drafted *St. Max* then turned to the other theatre idea uppermost in my mind – something that would reflect the influence of David Bowie on New Zealand and the impact of Bowie on me. I alternated between working on the two plays, but soon managed to get a slot at Bats Theatre to produce *The Temptations Of St. Max* with me as director. The reality of the upcoming production swung my attention onto *St. Max*, and *John, I'm Only Dancing* remained in a polished first-draft form.

After the season of *St. Max*, and having run through the Writers Bursary, I was drawn into other things – mainly writing television drama – and it was a few years before I came back to theatre, and then it was with another play.

John languished – sidelined but never forgotten by me. For a start, it's the play most drawn from my own experience. I'm not the character of Alan – or any of the characters – but let's face it, the setting is my high school in Rotorua; the environment, the vernacular and some of the events are taken from my experience of that school for four and a half years from 1973 to 1977. And anyone who was there with me is bound to recognise certain things.

As I wrote I pulled things up out of my memory, and of course invented or exaggerated others – but this play is real to me. It's set in a real place – I can see that narrow cluttered Prefects' Room, the corridor behind it, the hall behind that where the show would be performed on the stage flanked by names of old boys dead in the war, the principal's office . . .

It's a vanished time, and worth pointing out that my school was an anachronism even while I was there, but for me at least this play captures a slice of a particularly New Zealand past.

Then there was the Bowie thing. David Bowie was the big musical influence on me all through those years – and arguably ever since. Maybe it is because he's an ideas guy – he sees himself as an artist rather than a muso – and if you look at a lot of the people he's connected with over the years, Lou Reed, Iggy Pop, Brian Eno, the same could be said of them. Not musically talented myself, I related to Bowie's music as literature. I had been a huge reader as a kid, but music largely replaced that in my teens. And the centre of that music was the Bowie albums of the seventies, always unexpected, always conceptually pushing forward. I'd hear the advance single on the radio and think 'What's he doing now?' knowing that I had to – we all had to – catch up.

Ziggy Stardust is not my favourite David Bowie record – I would rate *Aladdin Sane*, *Diamond Dogs*, *Young Americans* or *Low* higher – but it was the one that kicked in the door. For glam, for stories, for concepts, for thinking. It proposed a new aesthetic that had nothing to do with Woodstock and everything to do with the future. It was as revolutionary an album as *Never Mind the Bollocks* would be five years later. The 'chameleon-like' (as he was unfailingly called) Bowie's ideas about fluid identity, making and re-making yourself amid the full spread of your personality's possibilities, was fascinating to me. Bowie was for the imagination, not against it – and I, unsatisfied with who and where I was and itching to grow, embraced that with excitement. Everyone needs someone to open the window and show them the light.

The incongruity of closing my eyes and listening to *Aladdin Sane* (say), only to open them at the end and find myself in Rotorua, New Zealand, dodging through my week in something like a parody of *Tom Brown's Schooldays*, was weird, unmistakeable, and in retrospect unmistakeably the stuff of drama. Polarities, contradictions – as I've sometimes said, to write a play all you need is two ideas to rub together, but it's important that they do rub together. Between Bowie's visions and the conditions in which my school life was waged there was more than enough friction to make sparks fly.

I love the architecture of this play. The story seemed to fit together very naturally, which after the sweat and labour of *Blue Sky Boys* was an exciting relief – maybe I was actually getting better at this thing? I enjoyed and found satisfying the concept of the final night show unrolling before us as we gradually learn what has been, and is still, going on behind the scenes. And the split ending – in which John loses in the real world but triumphs in Ziggy-world. Also satisfying were the little things – like Jackson's discovery of reggae, marking the moment when the Jimi Hendrix mirrors and afros of Rotorua took an abrupt turn into the Caribbean.

The script published here – with a few tweaks and line edits – is not that far from the polished first draft of so long ago. It seemed to know what it wanted to be from the outset, and I've opted to let that be. It's strange to have a play whose life has been solely on the page (and in my head) for so many years – but I think it takes its natural place in this trilogy of 'music' plays.

One day I'll see *John, I'm Only Dancing* on stage I think. I only hope – after such a long delay – that it measures up to the production I've run so many times in my imagination. Mind you, by then you might be able to plug directly into my brain and download precisely that show in all its glory.

During my high school years, if David Bowie was one guide – sending messages through the ether like his own Starman – then I also had another, more earthbound, mentor: Thomas Francis Eugene Tague, my History teacher. The two men could not be more different. Tom's preferred music was Italian opera and Latin masses, but he also was a great man for thinking and questioning – and in his own way he too was a rebel (rebel). I will always be grateful to him for also opening a window and letting in the light. Tom died not too long ago, but I think he would have got a real laugh out of this play. So it's dedicated to him.

For Tom

JOHN, I'M ONLY DANCING

Characters

John Jamieson   –   Music Teacher

Stoat (Mr Chote)   –   Headmaster

Alan Spencer   –   Head Prefect

Jerry Holder   –   Deputy Head Prefect

Noddy Peterson   –   Second Year Sixth

Jackson Kingi   –   Fifth Former

Diane   –   Head Girl, Girls' High

Jenny   –   Senior, Girls' High

The scenes take place in chronological order across a period of about eight weeks. All the musical performances between scenes are as performed on the final night of the school show.

The school musical is on one level the story of the rise and fall of Ziggy Stardust as told on the album, but John Jamieson has also shaped and staged the presentation of the songs to tell his own story, a boy struggling with his philistine and antagonistic surroundings, discovering music, being drawn into a glittering wider world as he acknowledges himself and comes out as gay, only to find the feverish life of the 'scene' hollow and his loneliness and sense of alienation redoubled. At his moment of despair he finds the love, understanding and acceptance he has been searching for.

Part of John's visual imagery for the show is a transformation for its characters from the 'ordinary' world into a 'glam' world – costumes in Act 1 largely reflect the ordinary world (allowing minimal change for the dramatic scenes) and in Act 2 are glam (including make-up).

The music is played by a small band – notionally local musos John has managed to call in favours from. Jackson – as Weerdon Gilley – plays guitar in songs where appropriate.

ACT 1

Set: a small cramped school prefects' common room and a dressed stage area where the performances take place.

Darkness. A beat.

'Five Years' is performed by Diane, Jenny, Jackson and Alan in 'ordinary' costume except for Jackson in soldier's uniform.

Jimmy (played by Alan) is caught up in the grief and chaos as the world tilts out of control. Amidst intimations of his dead mother he seeks connection, but is closed out and left alone in the growing hysteria.

Scene 1: Beginning

Lights up on the Prefects' Room of a boys' secondary school, 1974. A Friday afternoon in early October.

Jerry and Noddy bang in, throwing down their schoolbags. An intelligent, ordered boy, Jerry wears senior uniform of grey trousers and blazer. As a second-year sixth, Noddy – scruffy, impulsive, a shrewd observer – could also be in senior uniform but chooses to continue wearing regulation shorts and jersey.

Jerry: Oh, piss off!

Noddy: It's true! Up on the stage. Behind the back curtain.

Jerry: A shit? A human turd?

Noddy: Not exactly human considering it's one of Dinsdale's. Probably been there for weeks.

Jerry: The teachers would have smelt it during assembly.

Noddy: Smelt it? They were probably close to chundering the whole time.

Jerry: Then why didn't they do something?

Noddy: I bet they thought it was old Blob. You know how he falls asleep in class and farts and snores in harmony.

Jerry: How do you know it was Dinsdale's?

Noddy: Man, I saw it. It looked just like him.

Jerry: He's the only one who'd have the nerve. Just getting up there and dropping one.

Noddy: He's an artist. It's his statement.

Jerry: You didn't tell Stoat it was Dinsdale?

Noddy: Fuck off! I wouldn't be able to sleep at night wondering where I was going to find a horrible shit.

Jerry: Alan caught him thieving off kids at the tuck shop again. But he was too scared to give him a detention.

Noddy: Alan never gives anyone a detention.

Jerry: Better than that prick Wilcox. He's up to sixty-something.

Noddy: Hiding behind trees and grabbing kids who ride their bikes past the 'Dismount' sign. What a man.

Noddy moves around restlessly. He stands at the door and sniffs.

Smell that?

Jerry: What?

Noddy: Friday afternoon electives. The smell of women.

Jerry: I thought you meant Dinsdale had struck again.

Noddy: So where's 75% ducked off to now?

Jerry: Over to Archery to see Diane.

Noddy: He's meant to be here. United front, right?

Jerry: Just to tell her we're going out to Earthquake Flat tonight to break the record.

Noddy: Not in that dunger of his.

Jerry: The Morrie eleven hundred land speed record is within our grasp.

Noddy: You just want Jenny within your grasp.

Jerry: Get stuffed.

Noddy: What'd you say to me? What'd you say?

Jerry: Fuck off, Noddy.

Noddy attacks him, pinching one of his nipples.

Noddy: Whistle! Whistle, whistle, whistle!

John Jamieson opens the door and looks in. Jerry and Noddy are instantly more formal.

John: Hi. Look I'll be with you in a minute – I've just got to get some stuff from the Music Room.

John – late twenties – is sharp, whiplike. He possesses a certain elegance, quickness of movement, and dresses with style for 1974.

Is Alan Spencer coming?

Jerry: He's just over at the Archery elective, sir. Should be on his way now.

John: See you in a minute then.

He goes. Noddy mimics.

Noddy: 'Is Alan Spencer coming?'

Noddy/Jerry: No, it's just the way he's standing!

Noddy nods in the direction of the disappeared Jamieson.

Noddy: Reckon he is?

Jerry: My brother Steve was a turd when Jamieson was in the sixth form. He says the whole school called him Tinkerbell. Used to razz him to shreds.

Noddy: And now he's back as a teacher.

Jerry: Bums to the wall, boys!

Noddy: Makes you wonder what he does with those recorders in the Music room. The big knobbly ones.

Jerry: Bass recorders.

Noddy: Arse recorders!

Jerry: Shut up – he'll be back in a second.

Noddy: Him and Dinsdale should get together. They could do a Concerto for Bumhole.

Noddy prances about playing an imaginary recorder out of his bum and singing 'Greensleeves'. He opens a locker – one with a picture of David Bowie taped to the front.

Jerry   And get out of Alan's locker.

Noddy: What are you going to do? Give me a detention?

Noddy takes a bottle of Bacardi from underneath the sports clothes and swigs from it.

Jerry: What the hell's that doing there?

Noddy: They're not going to check the Head Prefect's locker, are they? And even if they did they wouldn't do anything about it.

Jerry: If Stoat came in here now your arse wouldn't touch the ground.

Noddy: Fuck Stoat. Just a few more weeks to Accrediting – then I'm gone.

Jerry: I'll drink to that.

He takes the bottle and raises it to his mouth. The door is suddenly flung open. Jerry freezes, caught in plain sight. The doorway is empty. Then Alan steps in.

Alan: What are you dipshits doing?

Jerry: You bastard.

Noddy jumps on Alan from behind and wrestles him.

Alan: Get off, Noddy, you prick!

Noddy: Whistle, whistle, whistle!

Alan manages to throw Noddy off. Attractive, with an easy charm, Alan enjoys the knack of being popular with his own as well as with the powers that be. He wears the badge of Head Prefect naturally – without having to display actual leadership.

Alan: Have you seen Jamieson? Did you tell him?

Jerry: We waited for you.

Alan: We don't even know for sure it is about a show.

Jerry: New music teacher. End of year. What else is it going to be?

Noddy: Somebody's told him about bloody *Pirates of Penzance*.

Jerry: What did Diane say?

Alan: Wanted to know what the show was.

Jerry: About tonight. Are we picking her up? Or is she taking her old lady's car?

Alan looks uncomfortable.

Alan: We were only out at Earthquake Flat last week.

Jerry: You've given the Morrie a stoke since then. She's a whole new machine!

Alan: Diane said she'd rather stay home tonight.

Jerry shrugs.

Jerry: Fair enough.

Alan: So I'm going round to her place.

Jerry: Piker!

Alan: You guys can come too. Her olds are going out so we'll have the house to ourselves.

Jerry: Great – yeah – after five minutes you and Diane disappear into her bedroom. Leaving the rest of us to get pissed and play snooker all night.

This appeals to Noddy.

Noddy: Count me in!

He takes a swig of Bacardi.

Alan: Jenny's going to be there.

Jerry: What am I supposed to do? Wet myself?

Alan: Anyway, I've got a match tomorrow.

Noddy: Then you shouldn't be shagging. Don't you know anything about health and fitness?

Alan: Look, I'm going to Diane's alright? You can come with me or not.

Jerry: Who said I wasn't coming?

Alan: (*to Noddy*) And if you piss in their pool!

Noddy: I can't help it, I'm a socialist.

Alan: They keep asking why I won't go for a swim.

Jerry: Did you shave between your eyebrows again?

Alan: Piss off.

Noddy: Gizza feel.

He strokes between Alan's eyebrows.

Ohhh. Smooth.

Alan: Get fucked – there's nothing wrong with shaving between your eyebrows.

John has come in unnoticed.

John: Plucking's better. Avoids unsightly stubble.

Alan, Noddy and Jerry are caught off guard. Noddy surreptitiously pushes the Bacardi bottle out of sight.

Alan: You wanted to see us, sir?

John: No. Not 'sir'. John.

He puts down a cassette player and a rolled-up bundle encased in tissue paper. He takes out a pack of cigarettes.

Smoke? Don't worry – everyone's gone home. I saw the Head driving out the gate in that foul little red car of his half an hour ago.

Alan: I don't smoke.

John: Of course. First Fifteen and all that.

Jerry shakes his head.

Noddy: I'll have one. Ta.

John lights it for him. His lighter is always turned up to full so a six-inch flame leaps out of it. John lights his own and exhales slowly, looking around.

John: Years since I was in here.

Noddy: Were you a prefect? John.

John: Hardly. If I was in here it was for chastisement. Back when prefects could still belt kids.

Alan, Jerry and Noddy are unsettled by his habit of crossing the long established line between teachers and pupils. John moves about the room, in no hurry to come to the point. He looks at the record player and its small stack of records – including Hunky Dory, Pin-Ups, Aladdin Sane.

Alan: Look, if this is about –

John: Who's the Bowie fan?

He indicates the David Bowie picture.

Jerry: That's Alan's locker.

Noddy: I'm more of a Black Sabbath, Led Zep man myself.

John looks at Alan.

John: This should interest you then.

John punches play on the cassette recorder. A live performance of 'White Light/White Heat' comes out of the tinny speaker.

It's a bootleg of Ziggy's Last Stand. At the Hammersmith Odeon last year.

Alan: The last Ziggy concert?

John: It's not bad as they go. Comes straight off the mixing desk.

Alan: How'd you get it?

John: I was there.

Alan: It must've been incredible.

John draws on his cigarette.

John: I was thinking about it the other night. Thinking I'd do it here. For the end of year show.

Noddy: Ziggy Stardust?

John: Sorry, *Black Sabbath – The Musical* just doesn't crank my handle. I hear the three of you were in last year's effort – what was it?

Jerry: *Pirates of Penzance.* But look – that was a mistake.

Noddy: We got conned into doing it because Mr White was retiring.

Jerry: And the thing is we've got exams coming up.

Looking at Alan who is not pulling his weight.

And there's the cricket season.

Noddy: And we'd rather not look like a bunch of dicks two years running.

Alan: You mean do it like a rock opera?

John: Somewhat overblown terminology. But yes, if you like.

Alan: Who's going to play the music?

John: There's still a few people in town who owe me favours.

Jerry opens his mouth but John continues.

As far as costume goes I thought this would be a start – for a touch of authenticity.

He shakes out the bundle and holds it up. It's a glam Ziggy-era top – a tight striped jacket with science fiction shoulder pads, open down the chest.

It was one of Bowie's.

Noddy: Get off the grass!

John: Are you calling me a liar?

Alan: Jesus. I've got a poster of him wearing that.

John holds it out to Alan. Alan takes it.

Did he throw it into the crowd?

John: His designer, Freddie, was a friend of mine in London. He rescued it from the bin for me. You could still smell Bowie's sweat on it.

John watches Alan as he is tempted to smell the garment. Instead Noddy sticks his nose in it for a sniff.

Of course I washed it. One can go too far.

John resumes wandering. He looks at the name on a locker.

Wilcox. Is that the zipped-up little bastard I saw handing out detentions to kids for not pulling their socks up?

He opens the locker, takes a book out and idly flicks through it.

Jerry: Does Mr Chote know about this show?

Noddy: We've never had anything that wasn't Gilbert and Sullivan. Or *My Fair Lady*.

John has crossed to the window and is staring out.

John: Times have changed. When I was here we didn't call him Mr Chote. We called him The Stoat.

Alan: He'll never let you do it.

John: Then you've got nothing to lose, have you?

Jerry: All the same –

John: Look – what's the big deal? In all likelihood none of you are even good enough. All I'm asking you to do is audition, set an example for the other kids, show some support.

He picks up the Bowie records.

Or are these just window-dressing? Would you actually prefer to see the same old boring crap year after year? So you can sit on the sidelines and criticise? Instead of getting off your bums and actually doing something to make this place better?

They are sure there is a reply to this but they can't think of one. John concludes briskly.

Good. Tuesday afternoon in the Hall. Now don't let me hold you up from whatever Bacchanalian ritual you've got planned for tonight.

They pick up their bags and turn to the door.

You'll be needing this, won't you, Noddy?

John pulls the bottle of Bacardi out from the couch. Noddy takes it. Alan is last out the door.

Spencer.

John ejects the cassette.

Why don't you keep the tape?

Alan takes it. He exits. John stands, staring around himself for a moment, still holding Wilcox's book. He hawks and spits into the book, tosses it back in the locker. Lights down.

Performance: 'Soul Love'
Diane, Jerry and Alan in school uniform, Jackson in soldier's uniform as the statue.

A cemetery: A girl in front of a war memorial, she meets a boy, they kiss and entangle as Jimmy lays flowers on his mother's grave. The statue comes to life. The boy gets rough, Jimmy intercedes but is bashed down. The girl comforts him, but turns amorous. Jimmy can't respond and she rejects him. He is left staring at the war hero statue as it resumes its frozen pose.

Scene 2: Auditions

Prefects' Room, Tuesday afternoon. Jenny and Noddy enter. Jenny wears seventh form uniform of the local Girls' High. Bright, friendly, a good sidekick, there are also depths to her.

Noddy: You were fine. When you hit that last note I could hear dogs barking all over town.

Jenny: I should know better than to ask you.

She screws up her face.

Why did I sing that? 'Who Will Buy?' God.

Noddy: Come on, Jenny – you're bound to get in.

Jenny: As what? A spider from Mars?

Jerry follows them in.

Anyway, I thought you guys were never going in another show?

Noddy: Supposedly this is an empty gesture of support.

Jerry: Jamieson thinks if he leans on Alan long enough he'll do it.

Jenny: Alan loves David Bowie. He's got posters up all over his room. Oh, I've brought him a picture – from *Jackie* magazine.

(*off Noddy's look*) My sister gets it.

Noddy: The only reason he went in *Pirates* was so he wouldn't damage his chances of making Head Prefect. Stoat wanted a decent turnout for old Whitey's retirement and put the hard word on him.

Jenny: It'll be the same as last year – whatever Alan does the two of you will follow.

Noddy: Pathetic isn't it? I despise myself.

Jerry: I still can't believe Stoat's letting Jamieson do it.

Noddy: Maybe he's a secret Bowie fan.

(*sings*) This is Major Stoat to Deputy Headmaster Toady

My balls are floating in a most peculiar way-ay . . .

Jerry: I reckon Jamieson hasn't asked him.

Noddy: And your ugly face looks even more like my arse today-ay-ay

He has picked up his bag and now heads for the door.

See you later kids.

Jenny: Aren't you going to wait and see if you're picked for the show?

Noddy: I've done what Jamieson wanted – I exerted my vast influence and threatened three turds into auditioning. As far as I'm concerned that's me off the hook.

Jenny: You've got a really good voice when you want to sing properly.

Noddy: Persuade Jerry. He'll do it for you. Won't you, Jerry-boy?

Jenny: What are you going to do when we're rehearsing?

Noddy: Hang out with Alan.

Jenny: Diane wants him to do it.

Jerry: (*to Noddy*) Piker.

Noddy: Oh – Jerry? Could you help me with this bit of Science homework?

Noddy pinches Jerry's nipple savagely.

Whistle! Whistle! Whistle!

Jerry: Piss off!

Noddy: Amazing medical fact – you can't whistle if someone's pinching your tit.

Noddy goes.

Jerry: Idiot.

Jenny: Is he going to get UE this time?

Jerry: Yeah, he tries to hide it but he's really worked this year.

Jerry rises.

Jerry: I'm on locker bay duty.

Jenny: Jerry – what you were talking about before . . .

Jerry: It's ok. Another time.

Jenny: You will go in the show, won't you? It'll be fun.

> *Jerry goes out. Jenny sighs. She gets up and looks at the Bowie jacket which is hanging up. She tries it on. As she takes it off her hand brushes her breast. She pinches one nipple and whistles. Diane comes in.*

Diane: Forgotten the words?

> *Jenny turns, embarrassed.*

            What's the whistling for?

Jenny: Nervous I guess. How did you go?

Diane: He doesn't even seem to know what the girls' parts are.

> *Diane is head girl of her school. Confident, attractive and assertive, she knows what she wants and usually gets it.*

Jenny: Who was waiting after you?

Diane: Some fifth form kids. And Evelyn Flavell.

Jenny: If he likes her he must be deaf.

Diane: I don't care one way or the other.

Jenny: No, it'd be rank if we didn't get in. Especially as it's our last year.

Diane: I saw Jerry down the hall. What were you talking to him about?

Jenny: Nothing much.

> *Diane looks at her.*

            He asked me out again.

Diane: What did you say?

Jenny's expression says it all.

Diane: Jenny! It's only the movies for God's sake!

Jenny: Did you put him up to it? Did you tell him to ask me?

Diane: I just don't see what's wrong with him.

Jenny: There's nothing wrong with him. I don't want to go out with him, that's all.

Diane: But you're not going out with anyone.

Jenny: Is that a crime?

Diane: He's going to be Dux this year. Alan told me.

Jenny: Oh, well never mind going out – why don't we just get married?

Diane: You could drop him if someone better comes along.

Jenny: That's easier said than done.

Diane gives up.

Diane: We'll all go to the movies.

Jenny: I don't think Jerry will go now.

Diane: Of course he will.

(*sighs*) I suppose we'll have to have Noddy as well.

Jenny: Are you getting sick of me tagging around with you and Alan?

Diane: No. I just want you to have someone too.

The door opens and Jackson Kingi manoeuvres a guitar case through the doorway. Jackson is Maori. A fifth former, he wears the standard school uniform – shorts, shirt etc. His appearance is scruffy, shirt open at the collar revealing a bead necklace, his hair in an afro, and a silver stud in his nose. As well as the guitar case Jackson is carrying John's cassette player and a tape. He stops, seeing the girls.

Jackson: Oh. Mr Jamieson told me to come in here.

Diane: Are you auditioning for the show?

Jackson: Nuh. I'm in it.

As Diane and Jenny exchange a glance, Jackson flicks up the catches on the case and lifts out an elegant electric guitar.

Cool, eh? John said if I was in the show he'd give me a lend. I can even take it home.

Diane: John?

Jackson: Oh. Mr Jamieson. He's even got the Marshall amp for it and everything.

Jackson plays and sings a phrase of 'Stairway To Heaven', mainly to impress the girls.

Diane: Your sister used to be at our school didn't she? Dulcie?

Jackson nods.

She left halfway through last year. You remember her, Jenny?

Jenny: What's she doing now?

Jackson is reluctant to talk about it.

Jackson: Oh. She's living up north. Kaikohe.

Diane: Gone up north for a bit.

Jenny: For another bit.

Diane: She had a boy, didn't she?

Jackson ignores this by going into a snatch of 'Purple Haze', filling in with his voice for the lack of effects on the unplugged guitar. He pulls back self-consciously.

Jackson: Ehhh!

Jenny: What's that in your nose?

Jackson: Oh. It's silver, eh?

Diane: I didn't think you boys were even allowed to have your ears pierced?

Jackson: Nah, they made a rule about it. But they forgot to say anything about noses. Can't break a rule if they haven't made one.

Jackson picks up the tape and loads it into the cassette player.

Supposed to be learning these songs.

Jenny: Don't you need music?

Jackson: I'll just listen and pick them up.

Stoat appears in the doorway. His gimlet eye sweeps the room, coming to rest on the girls.

Stoat: I'm looking for Spencer.

Diane: Have you tried the auditions?

Stoat: You mean to say Spencer is interested in a role in this show of Mr Jamieson's?

Diane: He was in last year's.

Stoat: I hardly think the two are comparable.

The school belongs to Stoat. As headmaster he holds absolute sway. Aging, he still carries no fat but has the colouring of high blood pressure or suppressed rage. His nickname – Stoat – could come from any of his physical features, or simply be due to the fact that he is a deadly killer to those small enough to be counted as prey.

Kingi, what are you doing in here?

Jackson has his hand up to his face hiding the nose-stud.

Jackson: I –

Stoat: Are you reporting to the prefects for detention?

Jackson: No, sir, but –

Stoat: Then get out, boy!

Jackson: Sir.

Jackson rises, trying to juggle everything he has to carry and disguise his nose at the same time.

As Jackson tries to squeeze past him Stoat pounces.

Stoat: What is that thing in your nose, Kingi?

He makes Jackson's name sound like a term of abuse.

Jackson: It's a —

Stoat: Get it out immediately!

Jackson drops everything and tries to reach up his nose to free the stud, enraging Stoat further.

Not here! I don't want to have to watch you!

Jackson moves to pick everything up again.

And pull up your socks, boy! Tuck your shirt in!

He reaches over and grasps the leather and bead necklace, twisting it so Jackson is pulled towards him.

And this.

Jackson unties it.

One more thing, Kingi.

Stoat grasps him painfully by the hair.

Tomorrow morning I want to see you in my office with this hair cut. Do you understand?

Jackson: Yes sir.

Stoat releases him with a contemptuous flick.

Stoat: Now get out of my sight.

Jackson does. Stoat returns his attention to the girls.

And how does Mrs Mallard feel about her girls becoming involved in this 'production'?

Diane: She hasn't said anything to us.

Stoat: I may have to have a word to her about it.

He goes.

Jenny: If he talks the old Duck out of it . . .

Diane: No chance. She hates him as much as anyone.

John appears in the doorway.

John: What'd he want?

Diane: He was looking for Alan.

John looks down the corridor after Stoat.

John: He's just found him.

He watches for a moment suspiciously.

Diane: Well put us out of our misery. Are we in the show or not?

John turns to them, entering the room properly.

John: You come as a double act do you? Both or nothing?

A moment of doubt as Diane and Jenny glance at each other.

Alright. I think you can manage what I've got in mind.

Jenny: Neat!

Diane: Who else is in?

John: So far Jackson. You could say I'm still negotiating the other three parts.

Jenny: There's only going to be six of us?

Diane: Last year *Pirates Of Penzance* had fifty kids in it.

John: No doubt forty-five of whom should never have been let near the stage.

Diane: It went really well actually.

Jenny: You weren't here then, were you?

John: No, but I'm sure it was the same as every other amateurish badly-performed act of necrophilia on the corpse of Gilbert and Sullivan that this school and your school have seen fit to perpetrate over the years.

Diane: That's not fair!

John: Good. Because I'm not fair. I'm very particular. And this show – my show – is going to be different. It's going to blow every other school production you've ever seen right off the map.

Diane and Jenny are pulled up short by his intensity.

I want to be clear from the beginning. So there's no misunderstanding later. Ok?

The girls feel a thrill of nervous excitement.

Alan comes in. Diane jumps up to greet him.

Diane: We got in! I told you!

She kisses him.

It's going to be great!

Alan is simmering.

Alan: Stoat just pulled me up. Started going on about my 'duties' as Head Prefect, my exams, and my responsibilities to the First Eleven. He didn't think going in a show like this befits my position in the school.

John: He actually said 'befits'?

Alan: I could find better things to do than mouthing the twitterings of some pop singer. He called Bowie a pop singer!

John: So . . .

Alan: So you can count me in.

The girls congratulate him.

John: Count you in what?

Everyone looks at him, realising they may have presumed too much.

Alan: (*meekly*) Count me in – sir?

John relents and smiles. He moves to the door.

John: Come on then – let's hear what your harmonies are like. Where the hell's Jackson got to?

They exit noisily.

Performance: 'Moonage Daydream'
Alan in school uniform, Jerry and Noddy in nightmare rugby gear and outsize boots, Jackson dressed Hendrix-style, not glam, as Weerdon Gilley, Diane and Jenny with cloaks hiding their school uniforms.

A rugby field. Pursued and taunted by a Clockwork Orange-*style gang (Noddy and Jerry). Jimmy is first harangued, tackled, stripped, rucked – then defies his persecutors, puncturing their rugby ball. As they savagely beat him up, Weerdon Gilley (Jackson) and his backing-singers the Spiders (Diane and Jenny) appear to take Jimmy's side and drive the ogres away with Weerdon's guitar attack.*

Jimmy discovers friends and a defence of sorts in music.

Scene 3: Mid-week rehearsal

Afternoon, during rehearsal. John and Noddy (still in 'Moonage Daydream' costume) negotiate a costume rack through the door of the Prefects' Room.

Noddy: It's pretty cramped in here already. What if the prefects don't like you turning it into a dressing-room?

John: Tell them this is Art, and they can move their fat and no doubt spotty bums for it. And if they've got a problem with that, refer them to me.

(looks out the window impatiently) Come on!

He lights a cigarette.

Noddy: Mind if I bludge one?

John: Like hell! Your voice already sounds like a bullfrog's fart and we're only halfway through rehearsal.

Noddy: Christ, this is turning into a bloody army camp.

John: It's up to you, sunshine. If you want to sound like shit on opening night then get steadily worse.

Noddy: Yeah, yeah.

John is still looking out the window.

John: What time were they supposed to be finished?

Noddy: Four. But you know Stoat – he's a fanatic.

He joins John.

Hey, is it true it was you that set the hedge on fire over there?

John: Who told you that?

Noddy: My cousin. He reckons the fire engines came out and everything.

John: As far as I remember it was never established who was responsible.

Noddy: Come on – Stoat's not going to cane you for it now.

John: No? You should watch him when he has to talk to me. His fingers positively itch. Every time I bump into him in the corridor I expect him to start screaming, 'Jamieson! Where do you think you're going? Jamieson! To my office and fetch the cane! Run, boy!'

Noddy: On my last day I'm going straight up to him and tell him to go fuck himself sideways. Twice for good measure.

John: You think you will.

Noddy gestures out the window.

Noddy: You should have burnt it right along.

John: It was the middle of winter. It didn't take properly.

Noddy turns with a sly smile.

Noddy: So it was you then.

John: Why are you so interested?

Noddy shrugs.

Noddy: It's history. All the stories about people who've been here, passed down from generation to generation. Like the nicknames – Stoat, J. Mo, Toad, Bonehead –

John: Tinkerbell? So why do they call you Noddy?

Noddy: When I was in third form my best mate had really big ears. He left but it kind of stuck. I never minded it. It was nothing compared to what Cuntface Phillips had to put up with.

John: Cuntface –

Noddy: Phillips. Perfectly ordinary guy. Quite good looking actually. We were all sitting around one day talking about nicknames – all the worst ones you could get. And he says, 'Nah – I reckon the most horrible name you could ever be called is Cuntface.' From that moment on his life was stuffed.

I'm going to be a journalist. That's the only reason I'm doing sixth form again. You've got to have UE.

John: While I was here the only thing that made any sense to me was music. Suppose I've got Cliff to thank for that.

Noddy: Old Whitey?

John: Poor old guy. Every other prick just flicked spit-balls at him. Music period was like feeding-time at the zoo. Christ, imagine thirty-five years of that.

Noddy: But you liked him.

John: I could hide out in the Music Room. He taught me to read notation. Lent me instruments. Him and his wife used to have me round for meals. He told me I had talent. When nobody else gave a shit.

Noddy glances out the window.

Noddy: Hey, they're coming off.

John: About bloody time.

As John turns to leave Diane and Jenny come in.

John: I thought you'd gone.

Diane: We're waiting for Alan. He's giving us a ride home.

John: You're going to have a long wait then.

Diane: No, he's finished. They're just coming in now.

John: He's not finished with me. I'm buggered if I'm going to let cricket practice stuff up my rehearsal time.

Diane: It's not Alan's fault.

John: It's not my fault either.

          John goes.

Diane: He's such a smart bastard! So sarcastic!

Noddy: He's alright.

Diane: You don't even hear half the things he says to Jenny and me.

Noddy: Yeah he shoots his mouth off a bit. But he's only trying to get the best out of us.

Diane: It's alright for you. You boys have got all the good parts.

Noddy: You can have my parts any time you like.

Jenny: It's true. He's only interested in you guys.

Diane: Because he's a poof.

Noddy: Crap.

Diane: Everyone says it about him. And you can see.

Jenny: Our last show before we leave and all we get to do is stand up the back all the time.

Noddy: No-one knows where they're going to be standing yet!

Diane: I asked him why he was bothering to have us at all – and you know what he said?

Jenny: That Girls' High has got a better Music Department.

Diane: And this way he could borrow our new keyboards.

Noddy: He's having you on.

Jenny: Even that Jackson Kingi's got more than us. And he's never been in a show in his life.

Noddy: He's in his family's band.

Diane: Well, Alan's not staying. He can't. He's coming round to my place for dinner.

Alan enters in his cricket whites carrying his bat.

Alan: You'd think we were opening at Lords instead of going down the road to play the tykes.

Noddy: Might that be due to the fact that St Pat's have killed us four years in a row?

Diane: Hurry up and get changed. I've got to get some vegetables for dinner.

Alan: John wants me to stay and do an hour's rehearsal.

Diane: What can you do by yourself?

John enters.

John: 'Star'. 'Hang On To Yourself'. 'Suffragette'. And the first half of 'Suicide'.

Diane: You can do that tomorrow. One day won't matter.

John: Every day matters.

Alan: I said I'll do it.

Diane: Well, how are we going to get home?

Alan: Take the Morrie. You can drop Jenny off.

He holds out the keys.

Diane: Then how are you going to get to my house?

John: I'll drop him off on my way.

Diane: Dinner'll be over by then. You don't expect Mum to hold it up just for you, do you?

Alan: Jesus, Diane!

Diane: Alright. Don't come at all. I don't care!

Diane huffs out, followed by Jenny.

Alan: Shit!

Noddy takes the keys off him.

Noddy: I'll get them home.

(*dirty old man voice*) Come on girls, hop in my Morrie. I've got a bag of sweeties.

Noddy exits. Alan looks harrassed.

John: Don't look at me. Women trouble's not my speciality.

Alan throws his bat into the corner.

Tantrums now.

Alan: It's just –

John: What?

Alan: Hard! Balancing everything.

John: Oh, right. So you want me to make allowances for you? You want me to make it easy?

Alan: I didn't say that.

John: I bet you've had it sweet right along. Picked out from the third form as being 'prefect material'. You've probably never even been caned. Or just once – so you wouldn't feel left out. Some pathetic pretext like breaking bounds at lunchtime. You wouldn't have a clue what it's like to be some kids in this school. When I was here the Head Boy's name was Symes. Son of a doctor. Still in the Old Boys Association I see. He liked nothing better than to kick me round this room of a lunchtime. He'd ram my head in those filthy toilets out there and make me lick them.

Alan: That's horrible.

John: No, I liked it. It turned me on.

They look at each other.

Alan: Not wearing my cap.

John: What?

Alan: I got caned for not wearing my cap. In the fourth form. So I could put a notch on my belt. All the cool guys had them.

John snorts and relaxes. Alan starts to undress.

What was it like living in London?

John: Dirty. Crowded. Brilliant.

Alan: So why come back?

John: My mother died.

Alan: Like Jimmy. In the show.

John: She needed me. I was in London. She got sick. I was in London. She died. I came back from London. If that makes any sense.

Alan: How come you decided to stay?

John: I didn't. I haven't.

Alan: Then why get a job here?

John: Cliff arranged it when he retired. His one solitary last minute act of insurrection. Stoat obviously didn't recognise my name. Or by the time he did it was too late. I thought then he must be losing his grip.

Alan has stripped down to his underpants and cricket box. Instead of changing into his school clothes he reaches for the Bowie jacket and pulls it on.

Alan: Hey, how about this for a costume? Get some silver boots or something and –

He strikes a pose.

Ziggy! What do you reckon?

John: I'll tell you one thing.

Alan: What?

John: This must be your first attempt at cock teasing. Otherwise you'd be making a better job of it.

He gets up.

See you in the Hall in two minutes.

John exits.

Performance: 'Starman'

Noddy and Jenny play teens drawn together by mysterious messages, they're joined by Diane in the second verse. At first a light in the heavens, then a voice, the glittering Starman figure (Jerry in glam costume and make-up) materialises to bless them.

Scene 4: Failed dress rehearsal

Saturday afternoon, the week before opening. Jackson ducks into the Prefects' Room as if someone's after him. He frantically pushes his hair behind his ears and down his collar. It immediately pops back out. Hearing someone coming he jumps behind the door. Alan enters, carrying his cricket gear. To get to his locker he pulls the door back, startling both himself and Jackson.

Alan: Jesus!

Jackson: Fuck, man, I thought you were Stoat!

Alan: He went down to his office.

Jackson: He reckoned if I didn't get a haircut, he'd cut it himself. No way I'm getting a kina off that bastard!

Alan puts his cricket gear away.

Jackson: Jamieson's going to have your balls, man. You bombed out the whole dress rehearsal.

Alan: There was a chance we'd have to bat again.

Jackson: When he heard you weren't coming back I thought he was going to hit the roof. He went all white, and his voice got real quiet. And he started talking like this, sort of 'Very well. Let's work whatever Ziggy-less pieces we can find, shall we?' And he really put the razz on your girlfrend. All afternoon.

Alan: Where is he now?

Jackson: Probably gone home.

Alan: His car's still out the front.

Jackson shrugs.

Jackson: Didja win?

Alan: They thrashed us. Despite the turd we found in the cricket bag with a flag stuck in it saying 'Good Luck Boys' High'.

Jackson: You should have seen the one on Old Jock's tractor seat yesterday. All the kids in the Photography elective were taking snaps of it. Rude, man!

Alan picks up his bag ready to go. John comes in. He looks at Alan then Jackson.

John: It's coming along well, Jackson. Just remember to concentrate on what you're supposed to be playing. Never mind the tributes to the guitar greats.

Jackson: Sure you don't want some Hendrix, sir?

John: Positive. Now go home and practise.

Jackson goes. Alan sighs and puts his bag down.

Alan: Look, I'm sorry. It was –

John: You think I'm interested in excuses?

Alan: I was stuck there! I'm the captain! Stoat said the team needed me –

John: I needed you! Here! It was the dress rehearsal!

Alan: There was nothing I could do!

John: I had to fuck around pretending we were doing something useful, pretending we were getting somewhere!

Alan: What do you want from me?

John: Everything you've got! Or nothing!

Alan: I've had it with this! I've got you on my back! Stoat! Diane! Everyone after their piece of me!

John: Don't flatter yourself.

Alan: Out there I'm supposed to be Jockstrap Spencer the sports hero! Then it's this Head fucking Prefect 'let's show our appreciation in the usual way' crap! And now you –

John: '75% Spencer'. Did you know that's what Noddy calls you? Always just enough effort and no more – just enough looks, just enough talent so you can sit back and wait for it all to come to you. So you never have to commit! So you can stay a baby all your life! Knock-knock – anybody in there?

            Alan is white and trembling.

Alan: And what about you? Mr Joe Cool Call-me-John! You think you're not a teacher? You're as bad as the rest! Stoat or any of them! Get the Head Prefect up there in a dress! What a laugh!

John: So what do you want to do? Quit?

Alan: Fine! I quit! You can stick your Ziggy Stardust! Get someone else! Or get up there yourself! That's what you really want, isn't it?

John: Piss off then!

            John tears the Bowie picture off Alan's locker, screws it up and throws it at Alan.

            I should have known better than to trust white bread like you!

            Alan storms out. John curses. He turns to go out, but Stoat steps into the room.

Stoat: Spencer seems a little over-committed. I warned him about that.

John: Successful cricket match?

John has obviously heard the result. Stoat reddens.

Oh well – it's playing the game that counts, isn't it?

Stoat: Not that it was ever your game.

John: I fancied myself more as a rugby player.

Stoat: Yes, I recall your trial for the First Fifteen. On the wing, wasn't it? Somewhat out of the blue given you'd never played in the Grades.

John: No doubt you haven't come looking for me to reminisce about my illustrious sporting career.

Stoat: This 'show' you intend putting on.

John: More than intend, it opens on Wednesday.

Stoat: I understand you're bringing in outsiders to perform music – excluding members of our own school band.

John: This requires a bit more than bad renditions of the *Pink Panther* theme.

Stoat: It all seems rather unnecessary, given that our school shows have been perfectly adequate in the past. Under Mr White.

John: I guess you'll just have to put it down to my youth and enthusiasm. You know me – keen as mustard.

Stoat: I know you alright, Jamieson. And experience has taught me that people don't change.

John: You may not. Now, if that's all –

John moves towards the door.

Stoat: No, that is not all.

He takes a sheet of paper out of his pocket.

Stoat: Mr McLaren has taken an interest in some of your rehearsals over the last few days.

John: Your Christian right hand. And here was I thinking he was just cleaning out the trophy cabinet.

Stoat: He has brought to my attention a number of areas of concern.

John: Concern to who?

Stoat: He tells me that the 'songs' – if they can be described as such – for the most part contain simple-minded gibberish and nonsense –

John: Then you've got nothing to worry about, have you?

Stoat: Which at times, however, descends into vulgarity and some undesirable subjects.

John: Such as?

Stoat: Mr McLaren has been kind enough to prepare a list.

He hands John the sheet of paper. John looks at it.

John: Very thorough. They don't call him Toad for nothing.

Stoat: I will not have you criticising good and faithful teachers who have served this school well for years! I don't mind telling you that when Mr McLaren brought me this list I was frankly disgusted. I couldn't comprehend that a member of my staff could see fit to propagate this kind of filth.

John: What are you talking about?

Stoat points things out on the list.

Stoat: Open blasphemy.

John: Leper messiah?

Stoat: References to drug-taking and sexual misconduct.

John: Stoned love? He's talking about a war memorial, for God's sake.

Stoat: Incidents of violence, grotesque and deviant imagery –

John: And a queer threw up.

Stoat: – all culminating in a glorified invitation to kill yourself.

John: What?

Stoat: I want every one of those references excised from each and every performance of this piece of rubbish.

John: That's ridiculous!

Stoat: If not then the entire production will immediately be cancelled. And your employment at this school reviewed.

John: You'd like that, wouldn't you? Why else have you waited till now to give me this?

Stoat: You can count yourself lucky. It's only in view of the effort put in by the students, and the fact that the majority of them are seniors who've shown themselves to be relatively trustworthy –

John: This is stupid! There's not a kid in this school who hasn't thrashed the *Ziggy Stardust* record! They've heard all of this a thousand times!

Stoat: In addition we will be monitoring the volume level, which Mr McLaren feels could become offensively loud. As well as any costumes. I can assure you that Mrs Mallard will not countenance her girls appearing in any kind of skimpy or revealing get-up whatsoever.

John: Look, what's this – you've got a line right through 'Rock'n'Roll Suicide'.

Stoat: That song must be removed completely.

John: It's the climax of the whole show!

Stoat: I will not have the subject of suicide bandied about in a school production!

John: It's not about killing yourself – it's the opposite!

Stoat: It can only improve matters by making the whole barrel of nonsense shorter.

John: You haven't even heard it!

They eyeball each other. Stoat moves in close.

Stoat: Do you really imagine I don't know what you're trying to do? To this school? To its pupils? If I hear a whisper. Just one whisper.

Stoat turns and walks towards the door.

John: Two tries!

Stoat halts.

In that trial for the First Fifteen – I scored two tries. I was fast. I had a sidestep. None of those meat-axes could catch me.

Stoat holds the door, his back to John, listening.

I could have been one of the big men in the school. Finally got some respect. Some acceptance. But you weren't about to let that happen.

Stoat: The First Fifteen are the school's representatives. Everywhere – not only on the field. I wasn't about to invite any shenanigans.

John: Shenanigans! I had so many sprig marks you could have played dominoes on me! But I didn't care. I was so stupid, I still thought I could get in. Get on the inside.

Stoat: On the day of the selection there was an act of arson on school property.

John: You made my life hell from day one.

Stoat: You didn't belong here. And as I said – people don't change.

He exits. Almost sobbing with frustration, John starts to trash the room, kicking the furniture over and tearing things off the wall. He is behind the door when Alan enters to get his bag which he has forgotten. John jumps on him from behind. Alan struggles, assuming it's Noddy.

Alan: Fuck off, Noddy!

The bigger and stronger Alan breaks John's grip and throws him off. John crashes into the wall. Alan sees it's him. They stare at each other. John grabs Alan. The moment is clearly sexual.

John: If you don't like it, then run.

Alan looks at him then turns to the door. Instead of going out, he closes the door and stands with his back to it looking at John. John moves towards him . . .

Performance: 'Star' / 'All The Young Dudes' / 'Star'

Jimmy is galvanised by the possibility of becoming a star. Weerdon Gilley and the Spiders are more interested in the money and fame. Stripping off the clothes of his old life, Jimmy is entranced and inspired by seeing a vision of the Starman in his mirror – who presents him with the Ziggy jacket. He puts the jacket on. With a lightning bolt of red lipstick slashed down his face, Jimmy is transformed into Ziggy Stardust. From the group chorus of 'Dudes' Jimmy / Ziggy returns to the last couplet of 'Star'.

END OF ACT 1

ACT 2

Performance: 'Lady Stardust'
Diane, Jenny and Alan – with backing by Jackson, Noddy and Jerry. All in
more exotic costume with make-up – Alan in Ziggy jacket and glam version
of tight blue jeans.

A dark club with shadowy decadent androgynous denizens. Ziggy is revealed.
Diane and Jenny are attracted to him as he first poses then sings on the chorus.
Jenny in particular is entranced, singing the 'smiled sadly' line. The other club
dwellers are steadily drawn into Ziggy's magnetism, recognising his star power.

Scene 5: Rescheduled dress rehearsal.

Noddy and Jerry bang into the Prefects' Room, wearing coats over their costumes.

Jerry: Crap. That is crap.

Noddy: I'm telling you, Jerry.

Jerry: You don't know what you're talking about. What've we stopped for this time anyway?

Noddy: Lights or something. They've overloaded the circuit. Look – I went past Jamieson's place last night. The Morrie was outside.

Jerry: All of a sudden it's 'Jamieson' again. What happened to 'John'?

Noddy: He's cool. He's fine. But there's a limit, you know?

Jerry: You'd better not be spreading this bullshit around.

Noddy: Yeah sure, like I'm going to tell the world that Alan's having it off with a man.

Jerry: He is not!

Noddy: I bet Stoat never thought to make up a rule for this. No fucking the teachers.

Jerry: That's not funny!

Noddy: Alright – this is a really weird thing to find out about one of your mates. But it's not just going to go away if you ignore it, Jerry.

Jackson ducks in quickly, wearing baggy white shorts and a football jersey.

Jackson: Man, why'd we have to do this dress rehearsal in school time?

Noddy: What the fuck do you want, Kingi?

Jackson: A place to hide. If my mates see what I've got on underneath here. . .

He illustrates.

Noddy: Piss off – we're busy.

Jackson: Get stuffed. You're not allowed in here either. You're not a prefect.

Noddy: I said fuck off!

Jerry restrains him.

Jerry: Leave it.

Jackson: Yeah, look out man, you'll mess up your lipstick.

Noddy: At least they don't have to put mine on with a trowel. Snapper-lips.

He turns to Jerry.

You should have seen Kingi's family band at my cousin's wedding last year. They've all got snapper-lips. A whole school of them.

Jackson: Fuck up.

Noddy: And talk about a groovy guitar sound.

(*he imitates*) Ka-joonga-jik. Ka-joonga-jik.

(*sings a snatch of 'Proud Mary'*)

Jackson: It's a job.

Noddy: Joong! She wears my ring-ng-ng-ng!

Jackson: We make two hundred bucks a night. That's more money than you'll ever see.

Noddy: Does that include the slut backup singer? Or was her performance out in the carpark extra?

Jackson: That's my sister, cunt!

Noddy: What does that mean? She gives you special rates?

Jackson jumps at Noddy and they fight, swearing and cursing. Jerry tries to intercede.

Jerry: Stop it, you bastards! Knock it off!

Stoat enters and, taking in the scene, puffs up with fury.

Stoat: Kingi! Get up, boy! You too, Peterson!

They scramble to their feet. Stoat grabs Jackson and hurls him towards the door.

To my office and fetch the cane! Second drawer of my desk! Move, boy!

Jackson goes. Stoat swings on Noddy.

Peterson!

Jerry: Noddy didn't start it, sir.

Stoat: I'm not interested in who started it! You're well aware this room is reserved for prefects. A little more attention to your studies last year and less hooligan behaviour might have meant you were one of them. As you are not, this room is out of bounds. Is that too complex a concept for you?

Noddy: No sir.

Stoat: Then get out!

Noddy is surprised, having expected to be caned.

Out of my sight, boy! Now!

Noddy realises that Jackson is going to get it, while he is let off.

Noddy: But – it was mainly my fault –

Stoat: What's that muck on your face?

Noddy: Make-up, sir. Stage make-up.

Jerry: We're in the middle of our dress rehearsal, sir. There's been a hold-up.

Noddy: Kingi's in it too, sir.

Stoat: Then I suggest, Peterson, that you get yourself back into the Hall and count yourself lucky.

Noddy hesitates, then summons his courage.

Noddy: If Kingi's going to be caned, I should be too.

Stoat: You're even more of an idiot than I took you for, Peterson.

John enters, with Alan close behind.

John: What's going on?

Stoat: A disciplinary matter, Mr Jamieson. Nothing that need concern you.

Noddy: It's Jackson.

Stoat: He'll be returned to you as soon as I've dealt with him.

John: We're in the middle of our final rehearsal. We need him to sing and play guitar.

Stoat: Neither of which he does with his backside I trust.

Noddy: It was my fault. I started it. I should –

Stoat: Shut up, Peterson! I'm sick of your whining! Get back to the Hall or find yourself suspended for insolence! Now!

John: Come on Noddy – everyone – back to the Hall.

Alan: What about Jackson?

John: It'll be worse if we stay. We're not the only ones putting on a show.

(to Stoat) Enjoy yourself.

John leads the reluctant Noddy out.

Jerry: Come on, Alan.

Alan shrugs him off. Jerry goes. Alan confronts Stoat.

Alan: It's this show you really want to get at, isn't it? It's John.

Stoat: Don't question me, Spencer. You have a position of responsibility within the school, be careful you don't abuse it.

Alan: What about you?

Stoat: That's enough!

Alan: What are you going to do? Cane me as well?

Stoat: Look at you, Spencer. Dressed in that ridiculous costume, looking like the town tart. The Head Prefect of this school! I've warned you more than once about Jamieson's influence. I can assure you he has neither the school's nor your interests in mind.

Alan: And you have?

Jackson enters, carrying Stoat's cane by the end.

Jackson: Sir –

Stoat: Give it here, Kingi.

He takes the cane.

Jackson: Sir, before you –

Stoat: I don't want to hear it, boy – bend down.

Jackson: But sir –

Stoat whacks the cane against the door angrily.

Stoat: I said bend down!

Jackson bends over. Stoat gives him six, which Jackson bears as stoically as he can. It's almost as bad for Alan whose rage and frustration grows, threatening to burst with each stroke.

I expect civilised conduct at this school, Kingi. Remember that.

Stoat turns to go.

Jackson: Sir, what I wanted to tell you was about your office, sir.

Stoat: What? What about my office?

Jackson: Well, sir, when I opened your drawer to get your cane out …

Stoat: Hurry up, boy! Don't waste my time!

Jackson: Well, sir, I saw someone had – done it – in your drawer.

Stoat: Done it? What are you talking about? Done what?

Jackson: You know, sir, done it. Tutae-ed. Crapped themselves.

Stoat: What!

Jackson: Yes sir, and it's all stuck to your papers and folders and things. And whoever it was rubbed the handle of your cane in it, sir.

Stoat looks at his cane and hand in horror.

Stoat: Good God!

Jackson: I tried to tell you, sir.

Stoat: Have you done this, Kingi? Is this you?

Jackson: No sir. I would have told you, but you didn't give me a chance.

Alan: That's right – you wouldn't listen.

Stoat is boiling with helpless frustration and disgust, and the urgent need to wash his hands and inspect the damage in his office. He breaks off and exits.

Stoat: Disgusting degenerate animals!

Alan and Jackson look at each other until they're sure he's gone. They burst out laughing. They laugh uproariously until Jackson's mood suddenly snaps and he rages.

Jackson: Fuckin' cunt! I hate this fuckin' place!

He is perilously close to tears. Alan looks at him, suddenly sober.

Alan: Yeah. So do I.

Lights down. Some music.

Scene 6: Second night pre-show

Flat light up on the performance area. Noddy comes on, looks out into the empty hall.

Noddy: (*sings*) Warm up – warm up – WARM UP!

> *He strikes a pose and sings a couple of lines of 'Time' – mimicking Bowie's accent – acting out falling wanking to the floor.*

What is 'wonking' anyway?

> *Jerry enters and steps over him.*

Jerry: Pommy version of wanking.

Noddy: Of course – Willy Wanker and His Chocolate Factory. That explains Milky Bars.

Jerry: I hear half of Eastern Valleys is coming tonight.

Noddy: Fame, Mama – at last!

Jerry: Second performances are supposed to be crap aren't they?

Noddy: Last night can make up for it. The best opening night this school's ever seen.

Jerry: Even finishing on 'Suffragette'?

Noddy: Just cos you miss your big number.

> *Jenny enters.*

Jenny: Jerry?

Noddy: (*acting unnerved*) Did you hear something then?

Jenny: Can we talk?

Noddy: There it is again!

Jerry: Noddy.

Noddy: I've got to paint my toenails anyway.

> *He exits.*

Jenny: Jerry – what's wrong with Alan?

Jerry: Wrong with him?

Jenny: Why's he avoiding Diane? Has he said anything to you?

Jerry: Like what?

Jenny: Diane's worried, Jerry.

Jerry: He's busy – that's all.

Jenny: He just disappeared from the party last night. She didn't have a clue where he'd gone. If you know something –

Jerry: I don't. For sure.

Jenny: Is it to do with John?

Jerry: What's it worth?

She moves closer.

Jenny: Jerry – ?

Jerry: I think you are truly beautiful.

Jerry kisses her.

Lights down.

Performance: 'Hang Onto Yourself'
Alan, Jackson, Diane and Jenny, everyone now in complete glam costume.

Concert. Ziggy and the Spiders in full flight, at their peak, flamboyant and ecstatic.

Jerry as the Starman figure appears fleetingly to Ziggy – a warning?

Scene 7: Second night post-show

The empty performance area. Lights slowly up on two figures kissing. Alan and John. Alan is still in costume.

John: You were great. Last night too. What time did you get home?

Alan: About two. Told my mother I fell asleep at Diane's.

John: Presumably she thought you were covering for a decent bit of heterosex.

Alan: This morning at breakfast she announces out of nowhere that an unwanted pregnancy can ruin your career.

John: Career? My God, don't tell me I'm finally going out with the man who'll support me.

Alan: She wants a lawyer in the family.

John: When I was your age all I had going for me was a clapped-out piano and a permanent hard-on. Of course I was never Head Boy.

Alan: Do you have to go on about that? Anyway, it's Head Prefect.

John: Head Boy sounds much better. Like some sort of erotic cartoon strip. Suckman and Headboy!

Alan tries to pull away. John won't let him.

Come on – lighten up.

He prods Alan, goading him until he reacts angrily and breaks away.

Alan: Knock it off!

John goes to Alan and pulls him to him.

John: I want you.

He takes Alan's hand.

Here. I want you to feel –

Alan: I already can.

John: My heart. Actually.

He places Alan's hand inside his shirt, over his heart.

It kills me to see you here in this dump all day. Where I can't touch you.

He places his hand over Alan's heart.

You know where the blood comes from when you get an erection? No-one knows. It's mysterious.

John: (*referring to before*) I'm sorry. I don't want to be like that with you. Just another queen with a smart mouth.

Alan: Very smart mouth.

John: Alan –

Alan: We're going to get locked in here if we're not careful.

John: Come to London with me.

Alan: London?

John: It's different there. It's alive.

Alan: I'm meant to be going to university.

John: There's a bigger world. With outrageous, extravagant, resplendent people. Over there you can be Bowie. I can be Bowie.

Alan: I suppose then Bowie will have to be someone else.

John: Sure it's all scene, everyone so busy knowing everyone they know no one. But for us it won't be like that. All you've got to do is forget this place and run. Like I did. Except you don't have to run alone.

Alan: You didn't forget this place.

John: I can now. With you.

Diane comes in.

Diane: I wondered whether I was getting a lift home with you?

John steps back.

Alan: Fine. Jenny too?

He starts to go out.

Diane: Alan.

A moment, then –

John: I'll check all the instruments are locked away. Don't be too long.

He goes.

Diane: What happened to you last night?

Alan: I wasn't in the mood. I would have told you I was going but you were busy.

Diane: It was my party – of course I was busy. Everyone thought we'd had a fight.

Alan: Everyone thinks all the time. You can't stop them.

Diane: He wasn't there either when I looked.

Alan: If you're talking about John I gave him a lift.

Diane: So you just dropped him off and went home?

Alan: We had a coffee. Talked about the show.

Diane: I wish he'd never come here. I wish I'd never heard of this show!

Alan: You're the one that wanted me to go in it.

Diane: I thought it was going to be fun. Like last year. It's not even a proper musical!

Alan: You think it should have stayed on the record player where it belonged?

Diane: Why are you acting like this?

Alan: Like what?

Diane: Like him! All smart and cryptic – pretending you're the same, when he's –

Alan: Queer?

Diane: And you're not!

Alan: According to Bowie everyone's a mixture. Partly man and partly woman.

Diane: That's just to sell more records.

Alan: He says you can be anything you want. Change yourself.

Diane: I don't want to change.

Alan: Just make up someone and become them. Like he's done.

Diane: Alan – please just tell me that everything is going to go back to normal – that we're going to go back to normal – once all this – (*gestures round the stage*) – is over. Alan?

Alan: I don't know.

Diane: What about next year – Victoria – getting a flat together?

Alan: I don't know.

Diane: What about us?

Alan doesn't reply.

This is him! He's done this! Bloody homo! I don't suppose anyone's told you how stupid you look?

Alan: Without my prefect's badge, you mean? Without my First Fifteen jersey?

Diane rushes out crying. Alan remains.

Lights down. Music.

Scene 8: Second-to-last night pre-show

Lights up on the Prefects' Room. Jackson is playing Bob Marley's 'Lively Up Yourself' on the cassette player. He is singing and grooving along to it. He interjects –

Jackson: Hey, hear this?

– before carrying on singing. John comes in from out in the corridor. He's edgy.

John: I hear it. But what the hell is it?

Jackson: Bob Marley. Far out, eh?

John: Sounds like it's being played on the wrong speed.

Jackson: Never heard of him till last week. Then I saw him on the TV.

John: What's the record called?

Jackson: Natty Dreadlock inna congo bongo I.

John: What does that mean?

Jackson: I dunno. But it's cool, eh?

            Alan enters.

John: You're late.

Alan: I know, I know. I fell asleep.

John: You haven't got time to warm up properly.

Alan: I warmed up in the car.

John: Have you tuned up yet, Jackson?

Jackson: Listen to this, man.

John: Then I suggest you get up to the stage.

            Jackson is absorbed in his music. John turns back to Alan.

            Just because I know why you fell asleep –

Alan: That you're the cause of it.

John: Doesn't change the fact that everyone has to pull their
            weight. Including you. Now, Jackson.

Alan: What is it with you? Isn't anything ever enough? Every
            night they're going apeshit over the show.

John: In its bowdlerised version – bad notes, dropped lines and all.

Alan: Nobody cares about that.

John: If all I'd wanted was a competent school show I could have
            wheeled out *Oliver!* and saved myself the trouble. Jackson!
            I said now!

Alan: I don't believe you sometimes.

            *Jackson heads for the door, singing. As he goes out Jenny enters. She
            crosses to Alan.*

Jenny: Alan, Diane would like to talk to you.

Alan: We said it all on the phone.

Jenny: She wants to see you face to face.

John: The show's about to start.

Jackson repeatedly sticks his head back in the door, still imitating Bob Marley.

Jackson: Hey, what you got in dat bag dere?

Jenny: She says she won't go on until you talk to her.

John: I'll talk to her.

Alan stops him.

Alan: No.

Jackson: No, what you got in dat other bag you got hanging dere?

John: Jackson!

Jenny is holding a picture. She proffers it.

Jenny: Bowie's new look. From the latest *Dolly*.

Alan takes it.

Alan: Short hair. And a suit.

He shows it to John who doesn't respond.

Jackson: What you say you got? I don't believe you!

John rises but Jackson is gone. Alan sticks the magazine page up on his locker.

Jenny: Alan, you've been together two years. She deserves more than a phone call.

Alan knows she's right.

John: It's five minutes to beginners!

Alan: It'll be alright.

Alan leaves. John looks at Jenny.

John: Set on sabotage is she?

Jenny: She just wants to talk to him.

John: And what do you want, Jenny?

Jenny: I'm sorry?

John: Always so quiet, always running messages for Diane. I understand Jerry's keen on you.

Jenny: Not really.

John: I've watched him. He positively salivates when you're around.

Jenny: No he doesn't.

John: Spontaneously ejaculates for all I know.

Jenny: That's horrible!

John: But he's not getting so much as a sniff off you, is he? What's the problem? Saving yourself?

Jenny: You're just being disgusting for the sake of it. You're always trying to stir people up.

John: I thought you might secretly fancy me.

Jenny: You?

John: Oh, I may not be a classic chip off the old two-by-four. But you'd be surprised the offers I get from women. They're always rubbing themselves up against me, standing too close when they ask for a light. Their stained teeth and their badly made-up faces.

Jenny: I'd better go.

As Jenny moves past him to the door, John slaps her arse.

John: Nice bum.

She turns and looks at him.

I don't trust you, Jenny.

She goes. John waits restlessly for a moment, looks at the picture of Bowie, feeling a worm of disquiet. He goes to the door and calls down the corridor.

Alan! Showtime! Let's go!

He exits in the direction Alan went.

Lights down.

Performance: *'Ziggy Stardust'*
Jackson as Weerdon Gilley, Diane and Jenny as the Spiders.

Ziggy appears in tableau behind them, corrupted by adulation, ego, riding on the devotion of the crowd (supplied by sfx). Ziggy feels hollow. He glimpses the Starman figure in the mirror, but it turns away from him. Frustrated, Ziggy smashes his guitar. He disappears.

Jackson, Diane and Jenny tear into the last verse. Jackson produces a thrilling guitar solo – even managing to inject a little reggae as he brings the song to a close.

Scene 9: Final night pre-show

Noddy and Alan enter the Prefects' Room.

Alan: It happens every year.

Noddy: I deserved to be Accredited! This time I'd earned it!

Alan: They let some through that they know will make the school look good in the results.

Noddy: No. It's Stoat. He couldn't have been happier when he caught me fighting with Kingi. Saved him having to change his mind about me. Five years I've been at this school.

Alan: (*sings*) Five years!

Noddy: And right up to the last minute he has to put the boot in.

Jackson appears wearing a rainbow knitted tea-cosy on his head.

Jackson: Hey, you fullas hear about Dinsdale? He's in hospital with a broken leg.

Alan: What happened?

Jackson: He fell off the front of the Main Block while he was trying to drop a turd on the school motto. Tripped up on his pants. Rude, eh?

Noddy: I guess Stoat's figured out who the Phantom Shitter is then.

Alan gestures at Jackson's headgear.

Alan: What the hell's that?

Jackson: It's my rasta hat. Like Bob Marley wears.

Noddy: It's a tea-cosy.

Jackson: Get off the grass, man. It's got all the rasta colours and it's for keeping my dread in.

Noddy snatches it off Jackson's head and looks inside.

Noddy: Man, there's like a whole city of kooties in here.

Alan: To keep your what in?

Jackson: Dread. Dreadlocks. Hair.

Noddy: If it's not a tea-cosy then how come there's a hole for the handle, and one for the spout?

He demonstrates with his fingers. Jackson grabs it back.

Jackson: Ok, it might have been a tea-cosy once. But now it's rastaman, just like Bob Marley.

Noddy: What happened to Jimi Hendrix?

Jackson: He died, man. Didn't you hear?

Noddy: At least he was better than that jungle beat you're playing now.

Jackson: You stick to your pakeha music. White bread like David Bowie.

Alan: There's no such thing as pakeha music.

Jackson: There is now.

Noddy: Hey, where's Jerry? He's usually the first one here.

Alan shrugs.

Did he say anything to you at electives?

Alan: He wagged it.

Noddy: Jerry wagged?

Jackson: Jamieson's not here either.

Noddy: He's gotta be here. He can't miss the last night.

Jackson: Not with what's going to happen.

Alan: Happen?

Jackson: That's right – you weren't here last night after the show. Jamieson was looking for you.

Noddy: You mean he hasn't talked to you about tonight? You haven't seen him?

Alan: I saw him this morning.

Jackson: He's a spastic, man. I went in the Music Room after lunch to get some new guitar strings. His fourth form class was wrecking the place. And he was just sitting there letting them.

Alan: So are you going to tell me? What about tonight?

There is a banging on the door. John's voice is heard from the other side.

John: (*off*) Ladies and gentlemen – from Los Angeles, California –

He throws the door open with a flourish.

– the Door!

He stands there – slightly shaky and unnaturally bright – dragging on the joint he is holding. Jackson is delighted by his temerity.

Jackson: Man, he's high! He's smoking dope in the school!

John: Unfortunately it doesn't noticeably improve the decor.

Alan watches, aware that much of this is for his benefit.

Anyone for a drag, said the queen?

Jackson reaches for the joint. John removes it.

No – maybe after.

He stubs it out.

Noddy: So – it's on for tonight then?

Alan: What is?

Noddy: 'Suicide'.

Jackson: 'Rock'n'Roll Suicide'!

Noddy: For the first time –

John: And the last.

Noddy: – we're gonna do it properly – the whole thing.

Jackson: Put all the other words back too.

(*sings a bowdlerised line of 'Moonage Daydream', replacing 'bitch' with 'witch'*)

Tiko!

Alan: Why?

John: To finish as we mean to go on. Intact. Unbowed.

Alan: It doesn't make any sense.

John: Tonight they see something. Tonight we want to be tight, hard and fast. As the actress said to the bishop.

Noddy: And Stoat can't do a thing to stop us.

He gives an imaginary Stoat the fingers with both hands.

Jackson: He'll never even know.

Alan: Of course he'll know. McLaren's here every night. And as soon as he tells Stoat you'll be down the road. He'll fire you.

John: What's the matter? Afraid you'll lose your dinky little badge?

Alan: It's just the excuse he's looking for. To never do a show like this again. I thought we were supposed to be changing things?

John: It's a bit late to try the rah-rah school spirit on me.

Alan: This is what you've planned all along, isn't it? One big scene – for the last night. The night when all the invites come.

Who's out there? The Board of Governors – the Old Boys Association – that Head Prefect who gave you such a hard time? They're all here, aren't they?

John: Alan, whatever you've . . . [decided] . . . I need you for this.

Alan turns to the others.

Alan: Are you just going to let him do it again? Get you jumping for what he wants? For his big moment?

John touches Alan.

John: They – wouldn't ever – look at me. Please . . . help me make them look at me now?

Alan stares at him, then turns away. John tries to make the best of it.

Break a leg.

He exits.

Noddy: As the actress said to Dinsdale.

Lights down.
Music in the distance: 'Ziggy Stardust'.

Scene 10: Final night, during the show

Lights up on the empty Prefects' Room. From the Hall the sound of Jackson's performance of 'Ziggy Stardust' can be heard. The door opens and Jerry bursts in, chest heaving. He looks as if he is about to cry or be sick – but fights it down.

Noddy: (*off*) Jerry? Jerry!

He enters quickly.

What are you doing?

Jerry: What's it to you, fuckface?

Noddy: Charming.

Alan: (*from the doorway*) He's pissed.

Noddy stares at Jerry incredulously.

Noddy: Jerry? You can't be pissed now! There's two songs to go! You've got to do 'Rock'n'Roll Suicide' for Christ's sake!

Jerry: Says who?

Noddy: Jamieson!

Jerry: Fuck him. Fuck him up his pansy arse.

Alan: We owe him that much.

Jerry: You do it then. But I'm not his bum boy.

Alan: What?

Jerry: You heard.

Noddy: Jerry –

Jerry: Fuck up! Keep out of this.

Alan: (*to Noddy*) Go back up. Tell John it's alright.

Noddy exits.

I don't care what you think of me –

Jerry: I think you're a queer cunt, that's what I think.

Alan: But don't fuck up the show for everyone else.

Alan turns to go.

Jerry: You think she's converted you back? Well, you know what I say? Once a queer, always a queer.

Alan: You don't know what you're talking about, Jerry.

Jerry: I covered for you! Thanks to me she probably thinks all you and Jamieson did was hold hands and listen to records! Well what if I told her different?

Alan: I wouldn't if I was you.

Jerry: Of course I don't know whether you stick it up him or he sticks it up you. But I could tell her enough to make her want to puke!

Alan: She knows. We sat in the car half the night talking.

Jerry: Talking.

Alan: I told her everything.

Jerry presses.

Jerry: Just talking.

Alan can't meet his eye.

Alan: What do you think?

Jerry flings himself at Alan and they struggle. Jerry rips the Bowie jacket Alan is wearing.

Jerry: You bastard! You fucking bastard!

Alan knees Jerry and throws him off. Jerry hits the floor. He looks up at Alan.

Nothing sticks to you. Ever.

Alan exits. Jerry gets up. He goes to Alan's locker and pulls everything out until he finds Noddy's stash – this time a bottle of Coruba. He downs a substantial amount.

Lights down.

Performance: 'Suffragette City'
Alan, Noddy, Jackson, Diane and Jenny – with interference by Jerry.

Ziggy, constantly harrassed by his followers, steers towards a breakdown. Wherever he turns there are more demands, betrayals, no one he can trust.

Though not meant to be in the song, Jerry appears – staggering, brandishing the Coruba bottle. He bumps into the others, some accidentally, Alan on purpose. He drains the bottle and starts to pull off his costume. The others manage to push Jerry towards the wings – where John's arm comes out and yanks him offstage.

At the climax of the song Ziggy goes down, disappearing under a ruck of his fans/hangers-on as they turn against him.

Scene 11: Final night post-show

Prefects' Room. Jerry is lying flaked out on the couch in his underpants. He still has his hand on the wastepaper bin he has vomited into. Noddy comes in. He leans over Jerry.

Noddy: You prize wanker.

          Jerry groans and turns over.

          You're lucky, sunshine. If it wasn't for John everyone'd be in here looking to kick your arse.

          John enters. He is wearing Jerry's 'Starman' costume.

John: Can you get him home, Noddy?

Noddy: Yeah. He's got Mumsy's car.

          Noddy finds the keys. He picks up the empty bottle.

          And he's drunk all my Coruba. Bastard.

John: Come on Jerry, let's get you decent.

          He pulls Jerry up to sitting position and manoeuvres some of his clothes onto him.

Noddy: So much for the last-night party. It was supposed to be at Jerry's place.

          Noddy indicates John's cigarettes and lighter which are lying with his clothes.

          Hey show's over, right? Now can I bludge a smoke?

          Noddy lights a cigarette and plays with the lighter.

          You really think Stoat's going to give you the boot?

John: I always wanted to be expelled. Never quite managed it the first time.

Noddy: You're better off out of here anyway. Fuckin' place.

John: In twenty years you'll be back for a reunion, standing around with a lot of people you always hated bullshitting about how they were the best days of your life.

Noddy: See you there then.

He hoists Jerry up and supports him. He hesitates.

This can't be it. Can it? After all that?

The door opens, Alan is standing there.

Jerry says he's been a silly billy and he's off home for bye byes. Don't you, Jerry?

Noddy makes him nod like a puppet. Alan moves into the room. Noddy hesitates a moment in the doorway.

You know – I reckon this night should go down in history.

He drags Jerry out. Alan and John look at each other.

John: I'm sure there must be a joke about going down in history.

Alan holds out the Bowie jacket.

Keep it.

Alan: Sorry about Jerry ripping it.

John Keep it. Keep me.

Alan: John ...

John: What? You don't want me to grovel? You thought you could get out of this without having to watch me beg? Tough luck.

He moves closer.

I can't help it, Alan. I want you.

Alan: You don't want me.

John: No?

Alan: Not really me. Something, maybe, you wanted to be.

John: Who's this talking?

Alan: Me. It's me talking. Finally.

John: So it was all just a mistake, was it?

Alan: No, I'm glad. Grateful.

John: Then come with me. Or we could stay. Maybe go up North – be hippies for a while? Anything. Just – say.

Alan shakes his head.

Alan: I've got to get a job. Make some money for university.

John: You think being a lawyer's going to keep you straight? The saunas are full of them.

Alan: I made up my mind. I'm going to do Arts. English, maybe even some Music.

John: Another resolution arrived at in the back of the Morrie last night? I hope you stick to all of them.

Alan: Thanks.

John: I hope you're miserable.

Alan turns to go.

Alan. I'm sorry. Please. Don't go like this.

He takes hold of Alan.

For God's sake, I – [love you]

Jenny steps through the open door from where she has been standing just round the corner.

Jenny: It's time we were going, Alan. Remember we're getting up early.

John lets go. Alan moves to stand by Jenny.

Alan: We're going over to the beach for a week. To Jenny's parents' bach.

John: How very kiwi summer. It might snow where I am on Christmas Day. So, Jenny – it seems everything does come to those who wait. Fate wouldn't happen to have thrown you together at the same university, would it?

Jenny: I've applied for Teachers' College.

Alan: It's just down the road.

John: Ah.

Jenny: We'd ...

John: Yes. You'd better.

> *They turn to go.*

Have a good life. Not too many sleepless nights, Jenny.

> *Alan turns in the doorway.*

Alan: You were great tonight.

> *Alan and Jenny exit. John picks up the Bowie jacket and finishes Jerry's work, tearing it in half. He puts a cigarette in his mouth but can't find his lighter. Angrily he crushes the cigarette and throws it away. Stoat enters, a little flushed, eyes bright.*

John: I see McLaren wasted no time.

Stoat: You always were a fool. Too much given to the grand gesture.

John: Couldn't this wait until Monday morning? When you're sober?

Stoat: So predictable.

John: I'm really not in the mood –

Stoat: I'm not interested in seeing you Monday morning or any other morning! The only thing I want left of you in this school by then is your letter of resignation. You don't belong here. Never did.

John: Then where did I belong? Can you tell me that? Where was the school for me?

Stoat: You didn't really think you could make a difference, did you? With Spencer? Or anyone else?

> *John is surprised Stoat is aware of the situation with Alan.*

I know you. I know the way your mind works.

John: I'm happy to say I can't say the same for you.

Stoat hesitates.

Stoat: I'm not a dark planet. I do have – reasons –

John: Oh my God, you're not going to get conscience-stricken are you? On top of everything else I'm not going to sit here and listen as you drool on about how sorry you are for everyone's lives you wrecked.

Stoat: Your life for instance?

John: Yes! Why the fucking hell not my life?

Stoat: Look around yourself. All I've done is take scrappy, snivelling, dirty-minded boys and try to mould them into some semblance of men.

John scoffs.

Yes, men! Who can act responsibly, who can achieve a standard of decency, who can stand up not for what they want – not for petty everyday desires – but for what they believe in.

John: Stand up straight and keep your hands out of your pockets. Be blank and stupid and never mind what's tearing you up inside. You pathetic – paper-bag of a man – you've sat on your dried up branch here for twenty-odd years trying to make everyone else's life as arid as your own.

Stoat: Do you really think the streets are full of people cursing my name? I'm only the principal of a school they once went to. A vaguely remembered figure they once loved to hate. So why are you different? Why can't you leave it behind? Why come back?

John: Don't worry, I won't be back again. You can keep this place. You can rot in it for another twenty years.

John makes to leave.

Stoat: These are my last few weeks. I'm retiring. I won't announce it until after the year's finished.

John: Then why tell me?

Stoat: I want to know what you're going to do.

John: Do?

Stoat: I'm calling your bluff, Jamieson. I'm dismissing you. What are you going to do?

John: How should I know? Go back to Britain. I've still got job contacts –

Stoat: Don't be deliberately obtuse!

John just stares at him.

I never could do a thing with you.

He turns towards the door.

John: How was the Principals' Conference this year? In Auckland again wasn't it?

Stoat has stopped.

The first place I ran to after I left here. The big anonymous city. Everyone talked about this toilet up Dominion Road. The light bulbs were always smashed. Even now the sound of shoes crunching on broken glass . . . You saw all sorts in there – from suits to Santa Claus costumes. The old queens were right. 'Dearie, you'd be amazed at whose cock turns up in your hand.'

Stoat: If you have any thought of blackmail –

John: I don't want to blackmail you! I want to know how you could mark me out, torment me and, yes, drive me away from here – when all the time you were the same as me?

Stoat: I'm not the same as you. I know what I am. And I know what you are.

John: Well I must be a bit thick then. Because I can't tell the difference.

Stoat: You want to change the whole world to suit yourself. If you had your way you'd have every boy in this school a prancing nancy-boy.

John: You can talk about nancy-boys?

Stoat: You don't even know what it is to be a man. To shoulder a burden, to endure, to not make a self-indulgent public display of everything you feel, everything you are.

John: I'm not Batman! I don't have a secret life. I'm not homosexual in my off-hours. I am what I am.

Stoat: I knew what you were the moment I set eyes on you. So perversely proud of yourself. So determined to thrust it into everyone's face, to revel in it.

John: To be honest.

Stoat: I doubt you've ever had an honest emotion in your life. You've allowed a single part of yourself to take you over until all you are is that one thing. A queer.

John: There's a new word for it.

Stoat: I'm too old for new words.

John: Things are changing.

Stoat: Too late for me. And for you I dare say.

John: So you thought you'd do me a favour by whipping it out of me? Or was it yourself you were beating? Clubbing it down like you always had.

Stoat: I've had my work. My school – which I won't stand by and see undermined. Not by you. My wife – whom I love. My children. I've known only too well my failings – weaknesses – cowardices. But I hated those things in myself. And I fought against them. That is what a man does.

John: And you call me a husk. You're right – I've only managed to lay waste my life. But you – you've deliberately, slowly, killed yourself inside. Until all you've got is the shell of your good name. And you stand there trembling that I'm going to take that away from you.

The sound of sirens is heard in the distance. Stoat seems suddenly vulnerable.

Stoat: My – wife is ill. That's one of the reasons I'm retiring. She's not – strong – and any kind of shock –

John: Don't. Please don't. You've got nothing to fear from me. You're free to – drink yourself to death in peace.

Stoat: I . . . Thank you. John.

John: Don't call me that. It makes my flesh creep.

Stoat: I'm sorry we had to –

John: Look, what are you hanging around for? A blow job's out of the question, I'll tell you that right now.

The sirens have come closer and closer until suddenly both men are aware that they are in the school. The window is lit by flashing red lights and another yellowish orange glow.

Stoat: What – ?

He moves to the window and looks out.

Good God! It's the hedge! It's blazing from end to end!

He looks at John.

John: Well I've got an alibi.

Stoat rushes out. John watches the blaze through the window, not knowing whether to laugh or cry. Noddy sticks his head in the door.

Noddy: Oy!

He holds up John's lighter. Behind him – equally excited – is Jackson.

What'd I tell you? Down in history!

He tosses the lighter to John.

See you later, mate.

Jackson flashes the peace sign.

Jackson: Rasta!

They run off. John picks up the ruined Ziggy jacket, presses it to his face, breathing in the smell. He starts to sob.

Lights down.

Performance: 'Rock'n'Roll Suicide'

Dark street. The first half of the song is sung by a broken Ziggy. At the moment of his deepest despair, as he pulls the jacket off and goes to tear it in half (it already shows the rip Jerry made in it backstage), he is stopped by the Starman image appearing in the mirror. Starman, played by John standing in for the drunken Jerry, appeals to Ziggy, assuring him that he cares and that he is not alone. He smashes through the glass of the mirror to take Ziggy's hands in a final melding of dream image and reality.

The other performers gather, providing vocal backing, watching as the Starman returns to where he came from – taking Ziggy with him. United. Whole. Loved.

THE END

'John, I'm Only Dancing' can be played during curtain call, or as an encore.

WATERLOO SUNSET

INTRODUCTION

Waterloo Sunset is the dark jewel here. It takes place over a black night of cold Wellington southerly wind and rain, and there's an undoubted grimness of place and time that seeps into the characters' bones and relationships. Each of the six is damaged – one fatally – by the time the sun rises. But rise it does.

Waterloo Sunset was the second of four plays written in a sustained burst and produced in Wellington at the rate of one a year from 2000 to 2003. Deciding I wanted to return to writing for the theatre as my main focus, I knew that I would have to make some changes. I sold my apartment in town – it was in an old building where the boilers and roof were about to cost the body corporate (i.e. all of us) a fortune. I headed for a more rural life in a cottage in Plimmerton, which sometimes seemed to amount to a life spent waiting in queues at the Paremata roundabout. With a clear run it was 40 minutes from my door to pick up my kids. And then all the way back again.

But it was cheaper. I could scale back other kinds of work and concentrate on plays. It was five years since I'd written one. Who was I as a playwright now?

The initial answer was *Flipside*, which was produced in the small theatre at Circa in 2000. My first Circa production. Simon Bennett came down from Auckland to direct it, which was great. A happy experience – written about elsewhere. I stood on the scrubby front lawn of my dodgy cottage in Karehana Bay on a clear afternoon with the *Evening Post* review glowing in my hand and felt that all was right with my world.

While *Flipside* was still on at Circa I was congratulated by Shane Bosher – our lighting/sound operator (now director of Silo Theatre in Auckland) – on the fact that *Waterloo Sunset* had been programmed by Downstage Theatre for the following year. This was news to me. But good news.

I remember being at the public launch of the 2001 Downstage season and Murray Lynch saying the *Waterloo Sunset* script had 'knocked his socks off'. The upshot was I had premieres of two plays within about six months. I was back.

I actually can't remember a lot about the process of writing *Waterloo Sunset* – except that it was done on my new green iMac (bought with the money left over from selling city apartment and buying country cottage) on a strange scriptwriting package that I'd got from somewhere. It was written on the same large and battered desk that all my plays have been written on (with the exception of two this year on a veneer table in the Katherine Mansfield Room, where I am writing this to the accompaniment of jagged tearing thunder and the first real rain we've had in months) which has occupied eight different locations in the years since it came my way in a Theatre Department clear-out of their 93 Kelburn Parade space in 1984. I do remember that I would time the end of my day's writing so I could hurry down to the beach to watch the sunset – spectacular off Plimmerton at any time of year.

Was there a workshop? Yes, definitely we did something of that nature in the bar space at Downstage – I have one or two clear images of that. And I do recall being a little perturbed at how fast this script was going into production. In the past I'd had more time to ponder and tinker.

Jonathon Hendry directed – we'd known each other for a good fifteen years by that point, since meeting through doing Theatre courses at Victoria. Those courses (and there were only two of them back then) were great – everyone was in together, those who were interested in acting rubbing shoulders with others who wanted to be writers or directors. Without noticing it, and before the word was invented, a lot of networking went on. Twenty-five years later I still find myself working with different combinations of the classes of '84–'86.

This play is dark, said everyone. Too dark, said one or two who read the script, and perhaps more than one or two in the audience. But it also has humour, and playfulness, and most importantly out of the ashes comes hope – not of the happy-ever-after variety, more about real love containing the will to endure. It's about growing up, about being John Lydon rather than Sid Vicious.

Punk is the jumping-off point for *Waterloo Sunset* – but not really its central concern. In the end it turns out to be about a marriage, which surprised but gratified me when it emerged through the writing of the first draft. One review of the play thought the final scene following the climax of the fire was largely unnecessary. I thought it was the single most wrenching thing I'd ever written. I took the hint and cut the scene down to half its previous length – for the better (coming after the action climax you know you've only got so many minutes of audience attention left) – but it's still the scene that it's all about for me, that grips me every time. The one where I felt I did what all playwrights want to do at the end of a play – write out of my skin.

I was never a punk. But I was influenced by it. The music, obviously – and it was fantastic to get that fresh air and that accessibility blasting through, if not the airwaves of a slow-to-respond radio hegemony, then at least bedroom stereos the world over, including New Zealand.

I remember seeing Dylan Taite interviewing Johnny Rotten for New Zealand television – Johnny all scrunched up sitting against the railings of Buckingham Palace in a dirty old coat. Dylan: 'What's your opinion of all this?' – waving his hand at the tourists watching for a glimpse of Windsor. Johnny's once-heard-always-remembered whine: 'I don't know, my brains are not wiv me today-y'. When I finally arrived in front of Buckingham Palace myself many years later, for me the historic charm of the place was that it was the hallowed site of that Johnny Rotten interview.

I bought *Never Mind the Bollocks* while I was still at school in Rotorua. The girl in the record shop knew my brother and reported back my surprising – from their point of view, embarrassing – purchase. I'm not sure how many copies of *Bollocks* they were shifting at the time in my hometown. Then the floodgates opened and there was new music everywhere. Briefly punk could be anything you wanted it to be, before the term new wave was invented for bands with more complex lyrics who weren't always pedal to the metal. The Pistols fell apart, the Clash grew up and out. Soon there was a uniform for punk, and a shrinking number of bands who were accepted as 'real' punk.

New Zealand's first punk bands (that I remember) were the Scavengers and the Suburban Reptiles (and even the Reptiles were pretty arty and included Phil Judd) but I was far from the Auckland scene – and I suspect I would have found the whole thing a bit frightening anyway.

In 1978 I started university at Waikato, where there was a sprawling sunny green campus and a strong holdover of hippies. As new kids started coming along clutching Blondie, Boomtown Rats, Talking Heads, XTC, Patti Smith and Stiff Little Fingers albums, the two subcultures mingled freely. I floated somewhere in the middle, dressing in op-shop jackets and waistcoats, cutting my hair shorter (after years trying to evade hair regulations and grow it long at school) and jamming it straight up. My proudest moment was when the punkest guy on campus asked me how I got my hair to stick up (soap).

It was the age of transformations. I remember seeing Mi-Sex play the Hillcrest Tavern – a fantastic pressure-cooker of a show – before they left for Australia and future glory. As human dynamo Steve Gilpin climbed the speaker stacks and hung from the ceiling it was almost impossible to remember that this guy had been round for years as a laid-back long-haired singer with a Duane Allman moustache and a passion for Chevys who was constantly called upon to cover JJ Cale's 'Cocaine'. Identities were fluid. And then suddenly they weren't anymore – and those sitting on the punk chair when the music stopped were faced with a little bit of a problem.

Graduating from Waikato I moved to Wellington and a horrendous grey winter which included a royal wedding and blood on the streets as the Springboks did the rounds. In 1981 there were hard-core punks in Wellington, not many, because it was already five years after the British fact, but they were there. Small tribes of them. One bunch I can remember would emerge in the early afternoon on Lambton Quay from some squat back up towards the Terrace. Dressed in my suit on my miserable way to or from my job as a computer programmer I would eye them warily and want to be other than I was. Not be them necessarily, just out of the straitjacket I had tried on for size and felt lock behind me.

There were skinheads and bootboys too (don't ask me the difference) – I'd sometimes have to cross the street to avoid a household of them on the way up the hill to my flat in Hataitai. The broken glass and other debris in front of their place included the mangled cover of a Throbbing Gristle album for a week or two.

A story. After work one Friday – and in my programmer's suit – I went to see the Sex Pistols movie *The Great Rock'n'Roll Swindle*. It had just opened that day, there'd been a 2pm matinee and now I bolted up Willis Street in order to make the 5pm showing. I bought my ticket, went up the stairs to go in – and the manager was standing in the doorway (something I'd never seen before) in a state of alert watchfulness. He cast an eye over my suit and muttered 'I'd sit somewhere where you can get out in a hurry if I was you, mate.' I – quite naturally – enquired why. He spilled over – 'At the last session they wrecked the place! Kicked the seats to bits, smashed stuff everywhere – you should see the state of the women's toilets!' Nervously, I cast a glance around. There were two people way down the front of the auditorium, a couple over to one side, three at the back. I said, 'Well, it doesn't look like you're going to get many for this session.' He said, 'There were only eight at the last one!'

The evening show the next day – Saturday – was forcibly closed by the riot squad, who deployed with long batons, the first time they had been used since the Tour, and proof that there was no going back. That was Wellington, that was New Zealand, and that was punk, back then.

I got out of the programming job, went back to university (Victoria this time, and those Theatre courses) and started working on being a writer. A few years slipped by, the knots of punks calcified. The catch-cry of 'No Future' took on a hollow ring. Exactly where were they going? As the rest of us found a hundred things to make and do.

Some things in *Waterloo Sunset* are based on real events of the time. There was a guy known as Softballhead – I never knew him, I should make clear – who died of exposure after taking a late-night winter swim in Evans Bay under the influence of the drug DMA. He had been seriously running out of friends since he had set a lamb alight at a party. These two facts were the genesis of the character of Oik – plus a liberal splash of the tropes and traits of Sid Vicious (who was originally named Vicious as a joke which was only funny while he remained a danger solely to himself).

Then there are the streets of Wellington as I first knew them – before the surge in inner-city living – dark and deserted after 6pm on a weeknight, windswept and rainy. On one such dark evening, on my way to the bus-stop in Courtenay Place from my aikido class in the rambling rotting sweat-smelling old YMCA up Willis Street (take up a new interest, join something), I passed the lit-up State Opera House, on the spur of the moment bought a ticket and watched *Foreskin's Lament* from a cheap seat in the gods, feeling the force of the drama as if I was in the front row. Just as with the punks, I watched and yearned to be other than I was.

With *Waterloo Sunset*, I wanted to revisit that ghost-town, and that pivot in history. Though the play is set a year before I took up residence (in some sense representing the rising wave that would break over our heads in 1981) and is physically contained within the walls of a boatshed, outside lies Wellington as I knew it then – the time and place I wanted to evoke – and I at least can feel that disappeared city as strongly as if it was onstage.

And then there's Rebecca – and the Londoners' Club.

Rebecca Rodden was my co-writer on the first four plays I had produced. I met her, yes, in a Theatre course at Victoria. She was a punk. I was not. She was also smart, funny, outrageous and a charismatic actor. We wrote things together so she could act in them. First a one-woman show for her, *Polythene Pam*. Then *Truelove* – so we could put on a double-bill at Bats Theatre. Then *Flybaby*, part of a triple-bill the following year (alongside a play by Gary Henderson and one by Leonard Cohen). Then our first full-length play *Jism*, written for Rebecca and Carol Smith to play Siamese twin sisters. Carol got into Drama School and Rebecca's disintegrating hip (from a bike accident years before) meant she couldn't play the part. We worked together once again some years later with visiting British street-performer Petra Massey on *Panic!* – a one-woman show for Petra – but in between I wrote four plays by myself, and moved into TV writing. Then I came back to playwriting and wrote another four plays – again as sole author. One of which was *Waterloo Sunset*.

Only trouble is, it used as its setting a place that Rebecca had told me about. The Londoners' Club – a converted boatshed where English expats who'd come over in the sixties would gather. Their pining for the surroundings of home found an echo in the Wellington punks' interest in all things English – and an unlikely cross-generation connection was made. Rebecca used to go there as a young punk, taken by her boyfriend. As soon as she told me about it I was fascinated by the dramatic possibilities. It rolled around in my head for years until I knew I wanted to write a play about it.

So did Rebecca. I told her we'd write it together. We didn't. Instead I wrote it by myself.

I'd gone too far down the track thinking about it – I knew what I wanted to do. The club was only a setting. All of the characters, the situation, the speech, the stories (with the exception of the cherry docs story – sleeping with them on her pillow – which Rebecca had told me about) were mine. I had forgotten saying we'd write it together (some years had passed). Those were all my excuses.

And I had genuinely forgotten. If I hadn't I wouldn't have rung up Rebecca and gaily suggested coffee so she could tell me everything she could remember about the club. She froze. That was her experience, she had always intended to write about it, we were meant to do it together.

Difficult.

I was hot to trot. I had the story – my story, her setting – and if I'd wanted to co-write I could have stayed in TV. We didn't have coffee. Or if we did we didn't talk about the Londoners' Club. I wrote the play. Beyond the setting (which I reasoned anyone could have told me about, and didn't belong solely to Rebecca) and the cherry docs story (all of a few lines long), I was confident there was nothing of Rebecca's in my play. She was not mollified. Her position was, I could write anything in the world, why did I have to steal from her?

Short answer – because the train was on the creative track. The juices were running. I sensed the power of this play, what it could be, what it tasted like – I was in excited pursuit, feeling I was in the right place doing the right thing. Right thing for me, of course. But I couldn't (wouldn't) stop it, couldn't kill it before it came into being.

I was also of the opinion – and still am – that if the cherry doc was on the other foot, I would say, 'Go for it. Take whatever I gave you as a starting point and run with it.' There's room for a lot of writing in the world – write what you want and see what sticks. Her reply might have been that I was now 'established' and had opportunities she didn't.

What do I feel now? I breached etiquette. Unwittingly. And then I wouldn't go back. Bad form. Not a sin, not plagiarism or theft – but not my finest hour either. Selfishness, maybe. Single-mindedness, absolutely. Certainly not greed and lust for glory – this is Wellington theatre we're talking about, hello? I've always felt a strong responsibility to the thing, the work, the play – to give it birth, for lack of a better metaphor.

I can come to regret the hurt I've caused – but I can't be sorry about the baby.

We rehearsed at the Wellington Irish Society up a side-street off Cambridge Terrace. It was a young cast – and an enthusiastic one. Matt Wilson made an imposing Stormboy, Nikki McDonnell crossed naivety with bravado perfectly for Cat, Kelson Henderson was fantastic as Oik, Peter Daube found the steel inside Terry's decency, while Phil

Grieve caught the right balance of sinning and sinned against for Davey. Casting Julie was always going to be difficult, but Rima Te Wiata came up from Dunedin at short notice to do it, which was a godsend. She was brilliant in that role, capturing all the intelligence, sensuality, anger, pain and vulnerability which made Julie the most satisfying female character I'd written at that time. It's Julie's play in many ways – and Rima bestrode it every minute she was onstage.

The stage itself was built up high at what was usually the audience end of Downstage, totally transforming the space, and excavating a hole through into the downstairs bar in the process. Nicole Cosgrove's design and set brought the faded decaying boatshed to draughty life and never let us forget the cold black water beneath.

Of the three 'music' plays, this one has the least music and no performance or sing-a-long moments. Punk is present more as a culture on stage – dress, hair, attitude and speech – than as a music, but the music is always behind it, bleeding through the cracks. As is the ghost of another music and culture from the same place but a different time – mid-sixties mod. *Quadrophenia* by The Who was a big album for me when I was about seventeen, and much of my understanding of mod came from the songs on that, the album's storyline (vividly written by Pete Townshend and photographed by Ethan A. Russell in one of the best album booklets ever) and the subsequent film. It is the superficial similarities and deep differences between these two youth-worshipping cults which enables the generation gap between the two sets of characters in *Waterloo Sunset* to be first papered over, then to tear violently apart.

The problem of how to grow up, which world you belong to, is thrown into relief by the experience of English immigrants in their thirties. The past for these characters in the play is literally another country. And the boatshed, perched over water, provides a liminal space for their shared state of in-between-ness. Waterloo Quay, Waterloo Station – as the dawn breaks on one, the sun sets on the other. The Kinks' song is perfect in so many ways, reverberates so well with the play, that it ended up giving it its title. Ten years later, in the shadow of the play, if I hum the song I'm likely to change one word. Instead of 'river' I sing about Terry and Julie crossing over the water . . .

WATERLOO SUNSET

Downstage Theatre, 30 March–28 April 2001:

Peter Daube
Phil Grieve
Matt Wilson
Kelson Henderson
Nikki McDonnell
Rima Te Wiata
Jonathon Hendry (director)
Nicole Cosgrove (set design)
Lisa Maule (lighting design)
Alice Tinning (costume design)
Peter Edge (sound design)

For Rebecca

WATERLOO SUNSET

Characters

Terry –	33, a Pom
Julie –	32, a Pom
Stormboy –	20, a Punk
Oik –	18, a Punk
Davey –	33, a Pom
Cat –	16, a Punk

ACT 1

Night: 1980. The Brits Club

The top floor of a boatshed converted into an approximation of an English pub for the sake of its members – expatriate Britons. There is a bar, stools, some tables, posters and memorabilia, pint mugs on hooks beside names, a fridge and sink behind the bar, a jar of pickled eggs on the bar, a TV.

On one side we can see a little of the exterior, part of a flight of rickety wooden stairs rising steeply to a small landing and the door of the boatshed.

At the back of the room on this side is a door leading to a small alcove with the toilet off that again.

Behind the bar is a locked walk-in storage cupboard.

At the back on the other side of the bar is a locked door behind which are stairs going down to the bottom floor of the building.

At the far side of the room is a door leading to the unseen 'snug' – a small room which becomes the TV room for watching the Cup Final.

Sound of wind, gusts of rain, a Wellington southerly. Terry clatters up the stairs, unlocks the door and enters, arms full of beer, scarves, a football rattle. He tries to turn the light on with his elbow, can't, crosses in the dark to dump what he's carrying on the bar. He curses as he runs into a stool. He switches on a heater which glows orange in the gloom, then moves back to the door and flicks the light on. It is only when he goes to pick up the things from the bar that he sees the large Anarchy symbol spraypainted in black on the wall behind the bar. It stretches across the painted wall and a couple of travel posters of London Beefeaters etc.

Terry: Shit.

Terry picks up a couple of crushed beer cans from the bar.

Davey enters with an armload of booze and football regalia. He is wearing his traffic cop overcoat and his cap though otherwise out of uniform. He crosses straight to the door leading to the 'snug'.

Davey: *(glances at the heater)* There's optimistic. We'll be dragging that straight in here, mate.

He disappears into the snug. Terry quickly moves behind the bar for a general check. The padlock has been broken on the fridge. He tries the cupboard door which is still secure. Behind the bar, Terry comes up with more empty cans – then a paint splattered plastic bag. He looks at it – then quickly drops it into the rubbish as Davey returns –

Tell me again why we're not doing this in the toasty comfort of your front room?

Terry: Atmosphere.

Davey: *(looks round)* Atmosphere. And your missus.

Terry: Julie's alright.

Davey: You two been at it again?

Terry: No.

Davey: Go on!

Terry: Might've had a word – that's all.

Davey: Me is it? Not welcome.

Terry: She doesn't want a house-full –

Davey: House-full! Anyone else turns out tonight, I'll sing Amazing Bloody Grace.

Terry: Course they will.

Davey: Could've stayed at my own gaff and you come over to me. Save me getting blown off the bloody motorway.

Terry: Will you give over whinging?

Davey: Eh?

Terry: Whingers. You Poms are all the same.

Davey: I'll give you fucking Poms . . .

He cuffs at Terry and they spar –

Terry: None o'that. Bloody football hooligan.

Terry knocks Davey's cap off –

Davey: Oy!

They scuffle. Terry starts to sing the West Ham song and – still scuffling – Davey tries to drown him out with a rival Arsenal song as if they're on the terraces. Davey looks up and sees the Anarchy symbol.

Fucking hell.

(stares at it) Those little arseholes.

Terry: You don't know it was them.

Davey: Who else? That's fucking brazen, that is.

Terry looks uncomfortable.

And I bet that's only the start.

Davey moves towards the bar.

Terry: There's nothing missing.

Davey: *(zeroing in on the cans)* These just drank themselves, did they?

Terry: A few tins of lager, it's not worth –

Davey: It never is with you.

Terry: The cupboard's fine.

Davey: (*finding leverage marks*) They've tried it.

Terry: There's even beer still in the fridge.

Davey opens the fridge and pulls out a full flagon.

Davey: Yeah, they don't go to all the trouble of breaking in here to drink their own piss-water.

He shoves the flagon back into the fridge.

I'll give them fucking Anarchy. I told you. Julie told you and all. You're too bloody soft – that's your problem.

Terry: I'll talk to Boy.

Davey: Talk!

Terry: Yeah – talk. Without you shouting the odds, Davey. Alright?

Davey shrugs – backs down.

They're good lads.

Davey: (*grumbling*) They're yobs. Cracking on they're hard. They're cream puffs. Imagine them down Shepherds Bush, or the Elephant and Castle – they wouldn't last five minutes.

Terry: And I suppose you would, Reggie Kray. You're not talking to some dolly now. I know you're straight out of Stoke Newington, you great ponce.

Davey: (*grins*) Newington or not – it paid to be handy. Are we moving this telly?

Terry: Leave it awhile. It's half-hour till kick-off.

As Terry tidies up and climbs up to take down the defaced posters, Davey picks up his cap, dusts it off and hangs it behind the bar.

D'you sleep in that?

Davey: Can't leave it in the car – some prick's always looking to pinch one. Like these.

He pulls a police truncheon out of his coat pocket.

Terry: That's never traffic cop issue.

Davey: Got it off a PC I know. Reckons they'll be well tooled up if this rugby tour goes ahead –

Looping the leather thong round his wrist, he strikes out with the truncheon.

– while we'll still be out there kicking bums and knocking heads together to get a bit of respect.

Terry: If the Police are going to be stretched, maybe you could reapply?

Davey: Nah. Happy where I am. It's a man's life in the Traffic Cops.

Terry: Heads up.

He flips Davey a key. Davey unlocks the cupboard, takes out a couple of cans of Guinness, cracks one and sits at the bar.

Davey: Who're you expecting?

Terry: Colin said he'd be here. And Les and Mary – if they could get the kids minded this time of night. Didn't hear back from most of the crowd – but they know we're here. Hey – get this – Peter Grey bought one of those video machines in Singapore. Reckons he's going to kip through the whole match – watch it first thing tomorrow morning. Where's the bloody fun in that?

(pulling down the first poster) He must be doing alright. Come over a good three years after me and Jools –

Davey: See sense, Terry.

Terry moves on to the second poster

They don't want to come here no more. They don't feel at home.

Terry: Colin said he'd be here.

Davey: They're not comfortable round a bunch of kids with green hair and a safety pin jammed up every orifice.

Terry: It's a bit of colour.

Davey: What can they talk to them about? Eh? This was meant to be a home away from home. Where we could feel in the majority for once.

Terry brings down the second poster, leaving the black mid-section of the Anarchy symbol on the wall.

Terry: The kids are interested. They wanna know for when they go over.

Davey: Not one of them is going anywhere but down the dole office every Thursday. They're too lazy to do a stroke. Probably too lazy to fuck.

Terry: Davey, they're just kids. Like we were kids.

Davey: (*snorts*) Say what you like – we believed in hard work. You clocked in every Monday morning for the readies to keep the Lambretta on the road and the birds on the pull. And we looked sharp.

Terry: You?

Davey: We dressed sharp! No stinking ripped-up shit for us. And – call me a liar if you like, Terry, but it's a fact – to us the world was our fucking oyster. We were excited about life. We weren't doom and gloom about everything from nuclear fallout to testing hair shampoo on rabbits. That's what really gets on my tits – we pay them so they can moan about the world made by people who actually got off their arse and did something.

Terry: Time you got off your arse. Shift that heater. We'll warm up the little room.

Davey: Now you're starting to make sense.

Terry heads for the toilet.

Terry: 'I'm just going outside, I may be some time.'

Davey: Eh?

Terry: Captain Oates, you berk. Scott of the Antarctic.

Davey: You still into all that bollocks. Public school nancy boys.

Terry: Like to see Arsenal walk to the South Pole. Bet they complain if they have to cross the road to the team bus.

As Terry disappears to the toilet –

Davey: You wait – West Ham'll wish they were at the South Pole.

As Davey unplugs and carries the heater through to the snug, Stormboy and Cat (clutching a half-full flagon of cider) spill up the outside stairs. They are out of breath, Stormboy having pretty much dragged Cat the last few blocks. She collapses. He holds her up, anxious to get inside out of sight. He strains his eyes back into the darkness.

Stormboy: Oik!

Oik stumbles in, more exhausted even than Cat. Where Stormboy is tall, well built (even taller and more striking with his bottlebrush hair), Oik is a runt, sallow and unhealthy. Cat – at 16 – is a punk poster-girl, whose natural beauty is raised a notch by the stark setting of shaved/spiked/coloured hair and lurid make-up.

Inside.

But Oik is in no shape. He leans over the stairs and vomits. Cat shrinks away in disgust. Stormboy resignedly sits down and waits for Oik's racking spasms to subside. Cat catches her breath enough to ask a question.

Cat: What happened?

Sound of a siren a few blocks away. Stormboy stares into the dark but says nothing. Oik sits back, wiping his mouth, smearing vomit across his face.

Oik: Fuck this place. Don't wanna go here.

Stormboy: The cops'll be straight round the flat.

Cat: What'd he do?

Oik: I want the knife. Gimme my knife.

Stormboy: I chucked it.

Oik: Eh?

Stormboy: I threw it in a bin.

Oik: Which bin?

Stormboy: I told you you didn't need it! He just wanted the same as us – a good time –

Oik: You saw what happened.

Stormboy: I saw you start it.

Oik: Bullshit!

They eye each other.

Stormboy: Just get in there.

Stormboy opens the door. Cat goes in, Stormboy shoves Oik inside then follows. Davey comes out of the snug and sees them.

Davey: Forget something?

Stormboy: Eh?

Davey: Come back to pinch more booze, chuck more paint around?

Stormboy: I don't know what you're on about.

Davey: You think you can treat people like shit and get away with it – that's what I'm on about. It's all just fucking Anarchy, right?

He indicates the bold black remains of the Anarchy symbol. Oik stabs his fist in the air.

Oik: Anarchy!

Stormboy: I don't know nothing about that.

Davey: Like fuck.

Stormboy: Terry invited us –

Davey: And this is what he gets for it. I should kick all your arses.

As Davey moves closer, Stormboy steps forward to meet him.

Stormboy: Better start with me.

Oik defuses the situation by bending over and yanking his pants down.

Oik: You wanna kick my arse – here it is.

He waggles his white spotty bum.

Say hello to Mr Arsey. Like looking in a mirror isn't it, Mr Wanker . . .

Davey – who has smiled at this display – darkens and makes a move towards Oik. Stormboy blocks him. Before anything can happen, there's the sound of the toilet flushing and Terry walks out.

Terry: Hey up, the terraces are filling.

Stormboy: Alright, Terry?

Davey steps back.

Terry: Come for the big match, eh?

(*looks at the cider in Cat's hand*) Still on the scrumpy?

Cat: It's the only one I like the taste of.

Terry: Get some Fullers down you, girl – put some hair on your chest.

Cat: (*indicating the Anarchy symbol*) Like your new decorations.

Stormboy looks at Terry.

Stormboy: We alright then? For tonight?

Terry: Reckon we'll squeeze you in.

Davey exits to the snug in disgust.

Stormboy: (*indicates the graffiti*) Must have been that pack of wankers from Lower Hutt.

Terry: You're not hanging about with them anymore?

Stormboy: Nah. Weekend punks.

Terry: You see 'em, you tell 'em. Paint on the wall's one thing, but sticking it up your nose –

He picks the paint-splattered plastic out of the rubbish.

– they're going to rot their brain out in no time.

They stare at the bag.

Stormboy: Kid stuff. Must have been kids.

Terry: Any kid of mine tried this . . .

He shrugs and drops it back into the rubbish. He turns to Cat.

The Gunners or the Hammers?

Cat: Eh?

Terry: Who you barracking for?

Cat: What's barracking?

Terry: Supporting! In the F.A. Cup Final.

Cat: Is that soccer?

Terry: Soccer? That's football, girl! Most important match of the whole year!

Cat looks at Stormboy.

Cat: Do we really have to watch it?

Terry: 'Really have to . . .'? Come here – I'll give you some pointers.

(*as he leads her away*) Soon as you see Davey – give it the old 'Ham-mers [clap-clap clap] . . . Ham-mers [clap-clap-clap] . . . !

As soon as they've disappeared into the other room, Stormboy rounds on Oik.

Stormboy: You dickhead!

Oik: What?

Stormboy: (*indicates the Anarchy symbol*) If you'd got us thrown out –

Oik: Lookit this place.

Stormboy: We've got nowhere else we can go.

Oik: Stinks of desperate old people. Fuckin' old perverts.

Stormboy: (*serious*) How bad do you think it was?

Oik: Drooling about sex all the time. Crapping on about how they were just like us.

Stormboy grabs him.

He deserved it.

Stormboy snaps, raises a fist as if he's going to deck Oik – then breaks away, fighting for control. Oik sobers, watching Stormboy's back.

There wasn't much blood. It wasn't like – spurting.

Stormboy: Could have been a lung. Could have been his heart.

Oik: Nah . . .

Stormboy rounds on him.

Stormboy: You don't know, do you? You don't know!

Oik looks on the verge of apologising –

Oik: I . . .

– *but doesn't.*

It just happened, y'know. It just . . . happened.

Stormboy comes back to practicalities.

Stormboy: We've gotta stay here. The cops won't know where we are. Then . . .

Oik: Then what?

Stormboy looks at him. He doesn't know. Davey comes back in.

Davey: Right – kick-off in a quarter-hour. Give us a hand to bring a few chairs through.

Stormboy moves to help him shift the chairs – Oik doesn't.

Come on, sunshine – make yourself useful.

Oik snaps to attention.

Oik: Yes, Sar'nt-Major! No, Sar'nt-Major! Lick your bollocks, Sar'nt-Major!

Davey: I did a dance when they abolished National Service. But looking at you makes me think it was a good idea. Come on – heft the telly.

Davey lifts one end of the TV, Oik supports the other.

Arsenal takes the win, there'll be a North London population explosion. Cup Night's always shagging night.

(*to Stormboy*) Looks like you're the only one who's got your tottie laid on.

(*to Oik as the cord stretches from the socket*) Mind the cord you wally.

Oik balances the TV as he bends to unplug the set. Davey turns to Stormboy again.

Don't know how you manage it without getting snagged in all those safety pins. Wouldn't do for me, fucking a girl with no hair. Still, it's all a bit of gash isn't it?

Stormboy has listened to this grimly, rage rising. He lets the chairs fall. As he opens his mouth, however, Oik drops the TV set. It hits the floor with a crash and Davey jumps to avoid being caught under his end.

What the fuck're yer doing!

Oik: It slipped.

Davey: That's just fucking marvellous, innit?

Oik: It was heavy.

Davey: Clear off out of it, go on!

Terry and Cat come out to investigate as Davey plugs the TV in to check it.

Terry: What's up?

Davey: He's only dropped the telly.

Davey switches it on − nothing.

Oh, bloody shit. It's bollocksed.

Terry: Let's have a look . . .

Davey: Ten minutes to kick-off and it's fucked!

Terry: Let the dog see the rabbit.

He bends to the TV and fiddles with the switches, changing channels etc.

Cat: What about the big game? I wanna see it now.

Davey: You'll be seeing fuck-all thanks to Charles Atlas here.

Terry slams the top of the TV − nothing. He slams again.

Terry: It's the tube.

He stands up.

Davey: What now? We can head out to mine but we'll miss the first quarter.

Oik: Can we come?

Davey: You'd be bloody joking!

Terry: I'll ring Julie.

Davey: She'll go spare.

Terry: She'll be alright.

He picks up the phone on the bar and dials.

Davey: It's the middle of the bloody night.

Stormboy and Cat have retired to a table. Oik joins them. Stormboy gives him a look regarding the TV –

Oik: (*quietly*) You wanna stay. If you'd smacked him we'd be out.

As the phone is answered –

Terry: Love. Wake you up? Sorry. It's just we've got a problem with the telly down here.

Julie reacts to the prospect of them coming home.

No – no danger – we're settled in here. What I was thinking of though was the bedroom portable. Thing is – if I was to come and pick it up, by the time I got back we'd have missed some of the match.

Julie points out aspects of time, place and weather.

Yeah, I know you are, love. I know it is. Yeah . . .

(*sucks his teeth*) No – as you were. I'll pop back and pick it up myself.

(*goes to put the phone down*) Eh? What's that, love? Davey – is it raining?

Davey looks out the window and wavers his hand to say it still is a bit.

It's stopped, love.

Julie asks who else is there.

Cat, Oik, Boy . . . dead keen West Ham supporters.

The punks cheer. Terry listens, smiles.

You're a champion – what are you?

He grins at the reply and hangs up.

On her way.

Davey: Back to sleep I bet.

Terry: Let's have a drink, lubricate the old voicebox.

He opens a can, throws one to Stormboy, Davey and Oik. As they tear the tabs –

Davey: (*to Oik*) No problem keeping a grip on that.

Oik sings the chorus of the Stranglers' 'Get a Grip on Yourself' – and slam dances.

Load of bollocks.

Terry sings the first couple of lines of 'You'll Never Walk Alone'

Oik: That's the bollocks.

Terry continues, singing in a surprisingly good voice, with feeling. Davey joins in on the last lines.

Oik replies with the opening shout of the Clash song –

London's burning! London's burning – !

Terry starts 'The Streets Of London'. Davey joins in.

Cat noisily blasts into 'Sheena Is A Punk Rocker'.

Oik cuts through with the opening of 'Blank Generation'. Terry makes the connection and chimes in with the 'sensation' line from 'My Generation'. Davey picks up the cue and together they continue the Who song.

In an effort to drown them out, Stormboy tries 'Anarchy For The UK', Oik 'God Save The Queen', Cat 'Pretty Vacant' – which she manages to get the other two to join in.

Stormboy goes into the chorus of 'White Riot', pulling Cat and Oik in to add voice – then Oik leaps into the first verse of 'London's Burning', Cat and Stormboy joining in.

The two songs continue, contending with each other, Terry and Davey enjoying the defiant stance of 'My Generation' but coming to a slightly uncomfortable conclusion with the lyric about not getting old.

Stormboy starts to sing 'Streets Of London' in the staccato shouting rhythm of punk.

Davey: Hey – !

Terry joins in with a laugh – then the others till they're all pogo-ing their way through the chorus, ending with –

All: Oi! Oi! Oi! Oi!

Oik: Oi! Oi! Oi! Oi!

(jumping round) OI! OI! OI! OI!

Davey: Alright –

Oik: OI! OI! OI! OI!

Oik is leaping and twisting like a terrier jumping up in Davey's face.

Davey: Bloody oi oi. Where I come from there's skinheads who'd use you for arse paper.

Oik: OI! OI! OI! OI!

He crashes into some stools.

Stormboy: Oik . . .

Before Stormboy has to restrain the manic Oik, Terry steps in, throwing an arm round Oik's shoulders –

Terry: Come on, sunshine – you win. You win, you win, you win.

Terry hands him his can of beer, Oik drinks and head-butts the can.

You're a hard man – no doubt about it.

Davey: Oh aye – hard as nails.

Davey heads back into the other room. Cat has sat back down at the table. Oik slumps down across from her.

Terry: Boy – that scooter I was telling you about, my Vespa GS . . .

Terry crosses the room –

Terry: . . . found a couple of snaps.

– and takes a few old black and white photos from his jacket which Stormboy joins him to look at.

Along the promenade at Brighton. Bank holiday.

Stormboy: What's all the mirrors for?

Terry: I used that one to look behind me. And the other nineteen to impress the girls.

Stormboy squints at the photo.

Stormboy: Look like you've got a split lip.

Terry: Always a bit of aggro down there. That was half the reason we went.

Stormboy: That impress the girls, did it? Getting beaten up?

Terry: Beat up?

He tries to swipe the photo back; Stormboy evades.

Let me tell you – the other bloke wouldn't have wanted his photo taken afterwards.

Cat is trying to roll a cigarette – disrupted by Oik purloining in turn her papers, tobacco, matches . . . Stormboy looks at the next photo.

Marble Arch.

(next one) Behind Julie's head there – that's St. Pauls.

(smiles) London on a summer's day. Can't beat it. Almost summer now.

Stormboy: You serious – what you said about your brother?

Terry: He'd put you up. Till you got on your feet. He's a brickie. Reckons there's jobs going. Docklands, all that.

(looks at Stormboy) Good time to go.

Terry doesn't know just how good.

Terry: Saving those pennies?

Stormboy: On the dole?

Terry: That offer of a job's still open.

Stormboy: Going round with you in the van? Fixing toasters?

Terry: Not just toasters, smart-arse.

Stormboy: 'A complete range of home appliances'.

Terry: Hey – I'm my own boss.

Stormboy: So am I.

> *They look at each other – grin. At the table Oik is striking matches – watching them burn – aware of the effect on Cat . . .*

Terry: I mean it. Provided you didn't piss all your wages up against the wall, you could be on your way before you know it. Waterloo Quay all the way to Waterloo Station. Eh?

Stormboy: *(glances back at Oik and Cat)* Yeah – I'll see . . .

Terry: See, see, see. What are you – Spanish?

> *He goes to turn away –*

Stormboy: Terry . . .

> *(looking at the first photo again)* You ever get into anything – serious?

> *Oik stands a match up on the side of the box – and flicks it at Cat.*

Cat: Stop it.

Terry: How d'you mean?

Stormboy: *(shrugs, references photo)* Fights.

Terry: Once or twice found myself out of my league. Still here though.

> *Oik flicks another lit match at Cat. She jumps up, upsetting her tobacco.*

Cat: Stop it!

Oik: Baa!

Cat: You bastard!

Oik: Baa-aa!

Stormboy and Terry come across.

Terry: (*dropping a hand on Oik's shoulder*) Come on, Oik, Round
         Two with that telly. We can set the little one up on top of it.
         If you manage to get it all the way this time.

*Oik helps Terry pick up the TV and move it. Stormboy takes
Cat's hand to stop her from following them. She takes a swig of
cider and kisses him, pressing herself against him, shotgunning the
cider into his mouth. Oik – backing through the doorway with the
TV – watches this uncomfortably. He and Terry exit to the other
room. Stormboy pulls back from Cat.*

Stormboy: I'll call you a taxi.

Cat: No –

Stormboy: You can pick it up at the corner.

Cat: I wanna see the soccer. I wanna be with you.

She is more than a little drunk.

Stormboy: You're not going to last all night.

Cat: Try me.

She snuggles into him. He peels her off.

Stormboy: Your Mum'll call the cops. I don't want you getting in
         trouble.

Cat: She can get fucked. I'm moving out anyway.

Stormboy: I don't mean trouble with her.

Cat: I'm moving into the flat with you. Tell me I am.

Stormboy: I've told you –

Cat: Well how long does it take to think about it?

Stormboy breaks away. Cat nods in the direction of Oik.

Cat: If he doesn't like it, he can find somewhere else to live. Or we can.

Stormboy doesn't reply.

I'm just going to move in. I'll bring my stuff round tomorrow.

Stormboy: Stay away from the flat tomorrow.

Cat: Why?

Stormboy: Just stay away.

Cat: He's done something, hasn't he? Something else like that lamb. He needs a babysitter.

Stormboy: You don't like it – go home.

Cat: No!

Stormboy: [please] I want you to go home.

Cat: I'm your girlfriend! You won't even tell me what he's done!

Stormboy: He got in a fight.

Cat: So you had to help him.

Stormboy looks tortured. Cat glances at the Anarchy grafitti.

It was him that did that, wasn't it?

Stormboy: Cat . . . Cat, listen . . .

He wants to tell her, he needs to tell someone. She puts her arms around him.

Cat: Let's go back to the flat.

Stormboy: This guy – at the party . . .

Cat: We can find somewhere here. It'll be fun.

Stormboy: Listen –

Cat: Come on . . .

She pushes his hand up her skirt.

Cat: You want to don't you, Boy? Don't you?

She kisses him. Stormboy staggers around with her. He starts to sing the Dead Kennedys song 'Too Drunk To Fuck' –

Am not.

Stormboy lifts her as he starts to pogo, still singing. As she's jerked up and down, Cat begins to feel queasy.

Boy –

He keeps it up, spinning her round and round, now singing 'Sheena Is A Punk Rocker'.

Boy – don't – ! . . . Stop –

(*on the verge of being sick*) Stop!

Stormboy lets her go. She staggers, dizzy, over to where she can slump down.

You prick.

She swallows, groaning.

Stormboy: Can't be a punk if you don't like to pogo.

He grins, picks up Cat's tobacco and Zig-Zags and rolls a cigarette.

You don't want to move into the flat.

Cat looks at him.

You don't, Katy girl.

Cat: Don't call me that.

Stormboy: It's your name, isn't it?

Cat: And your name's not Boy – or Stormboy.

Stormboy holds the rollie up to her mouth. She hesitates, then accepts it. He places the matches in front of her.

Stormboy: You want to get out of home – fine. But there's a lot
              more places in the world than the flat.

Cat: You don't want me round. You think I'll embarrass you.

Stormboy grabs one of her feet and pulls it up.

Stormboy: What's this?

Cat: Let go.

Stormboy: (*tapping her boot*) I know how bad you wanted these –
how hard you worked to get them. The bullshit you gave
your Mum so you could scrape together the money. Cherry
Docs. That's all you could think about. Remember what you
told me about the first night you got them?

Cat: You're laughing at me.

She struggles to get her foot free – Stormboy holds on.

Stormboy: That first night –

Cat: Alright, so I slept with them on my pillow.

Stormboy: And you swore you'd keep them perfect, didn't you? Not
a scratch, not a scuff, shine them every day. Look at them,
they're still like new. If you died – right here tonight – you'd
want to be buried in them, wouldn't you? You'd want to be
lying in that coffin with these boots on.

Cat: No.

They'd be on the top. Where everyone could see them.

Stormboy: Cat's cherry docs.

Cat: And for the music I'd have Penetration. 'Life's A Gamble'.

Stormboy: (*drops her foot*) They're just a pair of boots.

She looks at him.

Just boots. What you wear on your feet. Everyone's gotta
wear something cos of prickles and stones and shit.

Cat: Did you take something at that party?

Stormboy: They're just a pair of boots!

Cat: You wanted me to get them!

Julie comes up the stairs to the open door unnoticed in time to take in the atmosphere between Stormboy and Cat.

Stormboy: Why d'you wanna be a punk, Katy?

Cat: It's Cat!

Julie walks in.

Julie: Mind if I come in?

Stormboy and Cat turn.

Stormboy: Terry's in back.

Julie doesn't move. She's wearing a coat over her nightie, shoes, but her legs are bare. She's smoking.

Julie: Give him a shout, will you?

Stormboy heads back towards the other room – Julie smiles at Cat.

Miserable bloody night. I've come straight out in my nightie.

Stormboy: (*at the door*) Terry –

He nods over his shoulder. Terry comes out, followed by Davey.

Terry: Hello sweetie.

(*doesn't see a TV*) Did you fetch it?

Julie: What'd your last nigger die of? In the car.

Terry: Magic.

As he heads out –

Davey: Need a hand?

Terry: (*exiting*) It's only a portable.

Oik appears in the doorway of the TV room.

Davey: Didn't expect to see you tonight, Jools.

Julie ignores him. Heading for the bar to flick ash off her cigarette, she turns her attention to Cat and Stormboy.

Julie: A cop pulled me over in Courtenay Place –

Davey: One of our mob?

Julie: (*doesn't look at him*) A proper policeman. Here's me thinking
                he's looking at the telly thinking I've burgled it – doing a
                runner in my nightie. So I'm burbling on about my old
                man, broken telly, F.A. Cup night – while he's hanging in
                the window with a grin all over his face. Cheeky bugger's
                looking at my tits the whole time.

                *She briefly shows the scoop neck of her nightie before pulling her coat
                round her again. Oik has drifted across to be on the landing outside
                the door as Terry comes back in carrying the small portable TV.*

Terry: Black and white 'n' all. Still – if we bunch up round it . . .

                He carries it through to the TV room.

Julie: Lucky there's not a crowd.

Davey: You stopping?

Julie: It's a free country.

Davey: If you're stopping I'll get you a drink.

                Julie glances at him.

Julie: I'm not stopping.

                *Oik makes his way quietly down the stairs and exits, as Julie looks
                sideways at Cat with the cider propped next to her.*

                You used to drinking that?

Cat: I like it.

Julie: That's an old man's drink, love. You want to watch out – you
                don't want that boyfriend of yours to wake up one morning
                next to some bald toothless old geezer.

Cat: Serve him right for sleeping with Davey.

                Julie laughs. Davey smiles a crooked smile.

Davey: Cheers, Julie.

Julie: Doesn't Terry need some help with his rabbit ears or something?

Davey: You're the one who needs some help.

He goes. Julie looks at Cat again.

Julie: I always meant to ask you. How d'you get your hair to stay up like that?

Cat: Soap. Sugar and water.

Julie: Didn't think it'd be hairspray. What about the colour?

Cat: (*shrugs*) Food colouring mostly.

Julie: Like baking a bloody cake. Suppose it takes all day.

Cat: There's fuck all else to do.

Stormboy: Oy –

Julie: (*to Stormboy*) Settle down – I've heard some language before. And it's just us girls, innit?

(*back to Cat*) Bet you look a fright in the morning. No worse than we did though. I used to wear a hairpiece, had the beehive and all for a while. False eyelashes, white lipstick, sooty eye make up – the full Dusty Springfield. I'd wake up of a Sunday morning, eyelashes crawling up my nose, looking like something out of a Hammer Horror . . .

Cat starts the chant Terry taught her.

Cat: Ham-mers! [clap-clap-clap] Ham-mers! [clap-clap-clap]

Julie stubs out her cigarette, takes another menthol out of a packet and lights it.

Julie: You can't tell me either of you are interested in the football.

Cat: Well there's fuck-all else to do.

Julie: Not what I would have said at your age. Terry and me – we could always think of something to do. And it was always the same thing.

She looks appraisingly at Cat.

Julie: What are you – seventeen?

Cat: Round about.

Julie: (*smiles*) Sixteen.

(*looks at Stormboy*) And you'd be . . .

Stormboy: How long you and Terry been married?

Julie: Year before we came out here – so it's . . . thirteen years. Lucky thirteen. I was twenty – Terry a year older. Even after we was married we couldn't keep our hands off each other. Terry's Mum reckoned it was indecent. We were living with his parents, see. Terry said he was going to tack the marriage licence up on the door of our bedroom where the old bag could see it.

(*taps ash*) Least we had a bed. The couple of years before that it was in cars, up right-of-ways, under the pier – you name it. Suppose we were lucky, really. Two years of going at it like rabbits, and no accidents. I reckon half the guests at our wedding thought I was in the club.

She looks at Cat.

It's funny, isn't it – here I am talking to you like this – you're young enough to be my daughter.

Cat: No I'm not.

Julie: Course y'are. I knew plenty of girls who had them at sixteen . . .

Cat: You're old enough to be my mother – that's all.

Julie stares evenly at Cat. Stormboy cringes. Terry comes out of the back room, as rain starts in heavy on the roof.

Terry: Teams on the paddock – let's be having yer!

Cat: Ham-mers! [clap-clap-clap] Ham-mers! [clap-clap-clap]

Terry: That's the stuff.

He winks at Julie as he shepherds Stormboy and Cat into the other room. Cat is still chanting and this is greeted with opposition from Davey. Terry comes back to Julie.

Come have a watch. You can sit on my knee.

Julie: That the real reason you got me down here?

Terry: We never used to miss one.

Julie: That was when they were in daylight.

Terry: First years here we'd sit up all hours to listen on the radio.

Julie: Didn't need my beauty sleep like I do now.

Terry: Quiet this year.

Stormboy comes back out.

Stormboy: You seen Oik?

Terry: *(shrugs)* The bog?

Stormboy goes to check the toilet. Terry looks at Julie.

Next year stay home, you and me in bed with the tranny, eh?

Stormboy crosses to the door, looking out.

It's hosing down, man. He'll turn up.

Stormboy doesn't turn. He goes out into the rain. Terry nods towards the TV room.

What d'you say, love?

Julie hesitates, but –

Julie: You go on.

Terry looks at her.

Terry: You alright?

Julie: I got here by myself. I can find my own way home.

Terry: I meant . . . is everything alright?

Julie stiffens, a little startled.

Julie: Course. Why?

Terry shrugs. He leans forward to kiss her.

You'll miss kick-off.

Julie turns the kiss into a peck, then turns away, fumbling for a cigarette. Terry crosses towards the TV room.

Terry.

He turns.

Just wanted to look at you.

He grins, disappears into the TV room. Julie turns back, fumbles to light the cigarette but she starts to fall apart. Sound of Davey and Terry singing along with 'God Save The Queen' Cat chiming in with the Sex Pistols' version as Julie takes the cigarette out of her mouth, places it with her lighter on the bar. She is sobbing, though there is little sound, mainly evident from the convulsions of her shoulders. After a moment, Stormboy comes back, soaked.

Stormboy: He hasn't come back?

Julie shakes her head, not looking at him. Stormboy heads for the toilet where he grabs paper towels in a largely futile effort to dry himself off. His hair in particular is wilting. Meanwhile Julie gets herself together, checks herself in the mirror of a compact she retrieves from her coat pocket and is still staring at herself, half-mesmerised when Stormboy comes back in.

I couldn't see him.

He stands at the door again briefly.

He wouldn't have gone far. Stupid . . .

He turns, looks at Julie who appears oblivious. He uses both hands to 'jam' his hair up into more creditable spikes, then heads towards the TV room.

Julie: Get me a drink, Boy.

Stormboy stops. Julie smiles.

I sound like a Southern Belle out of a film.

(*Gone With The Wind accent*) 'Fetch me a Mint Julep, boy – while I set out here on the porch swing.' Why do they call you Boy, Boy?

Stormboy: It's short for something.

Julie: Boyden? Boyce? Boyd?

Stormboy: I thought you weren't staying.

Julie: It's pissing down. I'd look like you do before I even got to the car.

Stormboy: It's warmer in there.

He nods towards the TV room where the tinny sound of the match commentary can be heard, suddenly accompanied by cranking of rattles and shouts as the game kicks off.

Julie: And noisier.

Stormboy hasn't moved.

If it's too much trouble . . .

Stormboy goes behind the bar.

Stormboy: What would you like?

Julie: Ohh . . . Bacardi and lime on the rocks with a twist.

(*smiles*) If I know what's in that cupboard – which I do – it's tins of Fullers and Tetleys. All with people's names on them.

Stormboy: (*looking in the cupboard*) Mmm – pickings are a bit thin.

(*looks at some tins*) 'Dean Colley'.

Julie: Ponce.

Stormboy: 'Harrison'.

Julie: He's a wally, she's as tight as a duck's bum.

Stormboy: 'Peter Gregson'.

Julie: That old soak. The only way he'd leave anything in there is if he died.

Stormboy: R.I.P. Peter then.

Julie: Telescopic arms. I sit on the other side of the table and he still gets his hand up my skirt.

Stormboy brings a third-full bottle out of the cupboard and shakes it dubiously.

Stormboy: Gimlet.

Julie: As you were.

Stormboy: There's always this –

He opens the fridge, pulls out and places on the bar the half gallon flagon of beer we saw earlier.

Julie: My – God. No Pom brought that in here.

Stormboy: We did. Last week.

Julie looks at it.

Julie: Perfect.

Stormboy: You serious?

Julie: What better to send me on my way.

Stormboy: You going somewhere?

Julie: Going home. Come on, mate – crack a slab.

Stormboy takes the top off the half-g and levers off the plastic cap.

Stormboy: It's 'scab'. Crack a scab.

Julie: Charming.

He pours her a glass and pushes it towards her. He re-caps the flagon.

Julie: Not having something?

He shakes his head.

You need warming up.

Stormboy moves out from behind the bar, heading for the TV room again.

Stormboy: Rain should ease up soon.

Julie: That copper who stopped me. Wanted to know if I'd seen any punks.

Stormboy stops, looks at her.

Stormboy: There's lots of punks.

Julie: You'd know I suppose. I wouldn't have said so. Not any more. Not ones like you. Girls with a hole in their tights maybe, boys with the haircut. Living somewhere nice, working somewhere nice, Design students . . . what's that name you've got for them?

Stormboy: Weekenders.

Julie: Weekend punks.

(finally lighting that cigarette) Ask me. What I said to the copper.

Stormboy: None of my business.

Julie: There used to be more of you, didn't there? When you first started coming here. It was a big thing then, wasn't it. Punk.

Stormboy says nothing.

I thought the Beatles would last forever.

Julie inhales, flicks ash.

She's sweet – your little punkette. Got a good figure. Can carry it off. No use being a porky little fat girl punk, is there? I used to have a body like hers. Though it might not look like it now.

Stormboy: Is this where I say you look fine to me?

Julie: (*smiles*) Is it?

Stormboy: Can't really tell with that coat on.

She crosses her legs, letting the coat fall open and her nightie ride up her legs.

And in your lovely nightie.

Julie: You've seen me before. Here. In a tight skirt. With all me make-up on.

Stormboy: You never hang round long, do you? Time we get here, you're usually on your way.

Julie: I have a laugh.

Stormboy: You don't really like this place.

She looks at him.

Julie: It's Terry's thing.

Julie turns towards the bar.

Anyway – cradle-snatching ain't yer? She's sixteen, what are you – ?

Stormboy: I've seen you somewhere else too.

Julie: Where's that?

Stormboy: Freyberg.

Julie looks curiously at him.

Julie: You don't look like a swimmer.

Stormboy: You do. When you're in the water. Impressive. The lengths you do.

Julie: The lengths I go to. What happens to your hair?

Stormboy: Goes all floppy. Looks like shit.

Julie: (*laughs*) No wonder I didn't recognise you.

Stormboy: You always look like you're in your own world anyway.

Julie: The bottom of one pool looks much like another, yeah? Could be anywhere. Any time.

Stormboy: I saw you meet someone there once.

Julie glances at him sharply.

Long time ago. Davey.

Julie holds his eye. He nods at the glass in front of her.

You going to drink that?

Julie: I didn't.

Stormboy: Didn't what?

Julie: Didn't tell the nice policeman with his nose in my cleavage that if he wanted to talk to punks, there were a few of them hiding out down the wharf in a manky old boatshed sometimes referred to as the Brits Club.

Stormboy considers this.

Thank you, Julie.

Stormboy: Thanks.

Julie leans forward fiercely.

Julie: You go in there right now and tell Terry you saw me with Davey for all I care! He'll tell you the score in more ways than one!

Stormboy: None of my business. I never told anyone.

Julie: Her?

Stormboy: No.

Julie: Your mates?

Stormboy: I only told you now.

Julie: Why?

Stormboy: (*shrugs*) Talking.

Julie: Talking …

She relaxes, brooding.

Julie: Talk some more, Boy-Boy. What have you been doing? Eh?

Stormboy says nothing.

You're in trouble.

Stormboy: It's just Boy.

Julie: (*nods*) Short for – [something]

Stormboy: Stormboy.

Julie: Stormboy?

Stormboy: It's a book.

Julie: Never heard of it.

Stormboy: Australian.

Julie: That explains it.

Stormboy: About a boy. And an injured pelican. It was my favourite book as a kid. When the movie came out I wanted to see it. Even though it was a kids movie. I went to the two o'clock session. This was three years ago, I'd just trained my hair up, dyed it green. Hadn't even got my Docs – just ripped-up sneakers and a suit from St. Vincent de Paul with paint splatters. Woman at the flicks wouldn't let us in, said we'd put the kids off. Everyone else wanted to see *Clockwork Orange* anyway. I told her I was going to protest, write to the papers, form a picket line outside. In the end I just walked in. When I came out, they all started calling me Stormboy. As a joke. Everyone else was Ronnie Rancid or some shit like that. I was Stormboy. It just got shortened.

Julie: And Cat – from Katherine?

Stormboy nods.

Oik?

Stormboy: Ike. From Isaac.

Julie: I always liked Isaac for a boy's name.

Stormboy: His father's Jewish. Arsehole. Threw him out of home at fifteen.

Julie: My name's not Julie, come to that. That's my second name – well, Julia. Doreen Julia. Always hated Doreen – and when I started going out with Terry he wanted it to be Terry and Julie like in the song.

Stormboy: Song?

Julie: The Kinks.

Stormboy shakes his head.

Come over here and that's the name that stuck. Terry and Julie. How was the film?

Stormboy: Not as good as the book.

Pause.

Julie: (*with a nod towards the TV room*) I hate him, you know.

Stormboy is not sure who she's talking about.

Davey. Always have. Everything about him just gets right on my tits. And then what do I do? I really let him on my tits.

She drinks.

It's like – you do everything that you can think of that's good to do. Then you run out. And one by one you start doing everything you can think of that's bad to do. To save you from doing nothing.

(*grips his arm*) And you haven't got a clue what I'm talking about, have you?

Stormboy: Maybe.

Julie: Maybe.

(*sits back*) Cos you're the last of the Mohicans. A vanishing tribe.

Stormboy: It was my birthday last Friday.

Julie: (*raises her glass*) Many happy returns.

Stormboy: Didn't tell anyone. Didn't want anyone to know.

Julie gets it.

Julie: You turned twenty.

Stormboy looks back at her levelly.

You're twenty. And you're still here. You were supposed to light your candles and use the same match for yourself.

(*with a certain amount of glee*) That was the big catch-cry – set myself on fire when I turn twenty!

Stormboy parries by singing the last line of 'My Generation' about dying before getting old.

Fair enough.

Difference is – we just hoped. You promised.

She stubs out her cigarette.

Cheer up – you'll get over it.

Stormboy shows no sign of having heard.

There is life on the other side, you know. It's just I'm not a good example of it.

Stormboy: (*staring into space*) Ever get the feeling you've been cheated?

Julie: Eh?

Stormboy: What Johnny Rotten said at the last Sex Pistols show. 'Ever get the feeling you've been cheated?' Rock'n'Roll Swindle. Cash from chaos. All that. What I wanna know – just cos it never pretended, cos it always admitted what it was – does that make it any less of a rip-off?

Julie: You can't take it too seriously.

Stormboy: What if it's too late to do anything else?

Julie: (*laughs*) Hark at you, Methuselah!

(*leans forward*) Listen – London's my hometown, yeah? I know where those kids came from. Your Johnny Whatsit, and the other one. All of them. I've seen the tower blocks. When they were talking about No Future – you take it from me, they weren't too far bloody wrong. Why d'you think Terry and I came out here, eh? Just for the sunshine? You haven't got a clue. Back there punks make sense. Here – I'm sorry – but it's a joke. Dress ups, innit? You're like this place –

She waves an arm around.

– pretending to be something it's not. No – it's not. Just the people inside it. Opposite to you, right? Poms. Poms who come here because they want some bloody corner of a foreign field that's forever England. What d'you think they're doing over here? You think if they loved England so bleeding much they wouldn't be there like a shot? Their England – the one they like to sit here and imagine – it doesn't exist! They go back there looking for it – on holiday, see the family – always thinking 'Well, p'raps we'll move back'. And they can't get out of there fast enough! They'll tell you it's changed. Arabs up Oxford Street, syringes down the precinct, always some excuse. No place for kids. Course it's bloody changed! Everywhere changes. Here's changed! You've got to change with it, right? You can't sit in one country and want to be in another, then when you're in that one want to be back where you started. I sit and I see them come in that door and it's like they're the bloody Flying Dutchman. Doomed to wander the seas and never touch land. 'Cept they're a sparky from Watford with a nice little business in Petone and an emergency parcel of pork pies every Christmas from their Mum and Dad. They're the cursed of this earth. Is that what you want?

She grabs his chin.

You're in your own country, you tosser!

Julie: (*takes his hand; more gently*) You're a kiwi kid. Only you can't be a kid no more.

Stormboy: 'When I became a man, I put away childish things'. Did that in Bible Class.

Julie: What're you doing hanging round with them? She's a child. Your ferrety little mate – he's never going to grow up. You can't spend your time with kids like you're still one of them.

Stormboy: Terry does. You are right now.

Julie: How d'you think I know?

She moves close to him.

Be a man. Not a Boy. Not even a Stormboy. Collecting waifs and strays with broken wings.

Stormboy: (*lost*) It's all fucked-up.

Julie: Don't be like Terry or Davey. Or me. Have the guts to grow up.

(*slips her hand in his belt*) What's so bad about being a man? Women look up to you. Not just girls. You want that, don't you? For me to look up to you?

Moment.

Yeah – well, that's the sermon for tonight.

She breaks away, packing up.

Time I was gone. Sling my hook. Vamos.

(*looking round*) Times I've thought about never having to see this place again . . .

Stormboy hasn't moved, has hardly seemed to be listening. As Julie heads for the door –

Stormboy: I killed someone.

Julie: What's that, love?

A wave of anguish crosses his face.

Stormboy: I think I killed someone.

> *Julie stares at him, trying to gauge the seriousness of what he's saying. The distress Stormboy has been holding back spills over in a rush of words –*

I didn't mean to. Oik got in a fight. I had to help him. But he pulled a knife.

Julie: Who did?

Stormboy: Oik. I told him he didn't need it. He went mad. This guy. Oik must have cut him. He went crazy, knocked it out of his hand. I grabbed it. I had to do something. If he'd got it, he would have killed him.

Julie: Who – ?

Stormboy: Killed Oik! Then he was coming for me. He was berserk. He wanted to kill me. If I'd let go –

> *He waves his hand back to where he somehow feels the guy is still lying.*

– it'd be me, not him!

Julie: Oh no.

Stormboy: He was kicking and punching, going for the knife. I put it where he couldn't get it. Straight in. Deep in. Like it was nothing. Nothing to stop it.

(*he feels his own chest*) I thought – bones . . . ribs. I must have got it between. A lucky shot. Beginner's luck.

> *He half-laughs.*

Julie: Oh, love . . .

> *She crosses to him.*

You've got to tell the police.

Stormboy: It's done now. I've done it.

Julie: It was self-defence, you were trying to break the fight up . . .

Stormboy starts to sob. Julie doesn't know what to do.

Come on. That won't do no good. Come on . . .

He keeps sobbing. Julie reaches for him suddenly and cradles him against her breast. He pushes inside her coat, clasping his arms round her. After a moment the embrace turns passionate. Julie's nightie is riding up and Stormboy's hands drop to her thighs. His body unwinds from his childlike hunch against her chest, kissing her, pulling her up with him as he stands, pulling her into him.

No –

He doesn't stop. His hand slips between her thighs.

Get your little girlfriend –

Stormboy: I want you.

He's mauling her, hands under her nightie. Julie starts to respond. They lurch back against the bar. Julie flicks a glance at the door to the TV room.

Julie: Here –

She pushes him across to the door to the toilet. He piles into the little passageway behind her, pressing her into the wall.

Come on then, Kiwi boy. Come on –

She reaches out and pushes the door closed with a bang. Almost immediately comes a burst of noise from the TV room –

Terry/Cat: (*off, shouting*) GOAL! GOAL!!

The clamour of celebration and goading of Davey continues as Oik staggers up the stairs. As he comes into the light we see one side of his face is covered in blood from a gash above his hairline. Blood has splashed down his clothes. His hands are bloody and he clutches his side. He wavers a moment, spits out blood then turns towards the toilet and pulls the door open. Julie is pressed face-first against the wall, Stormboy fucking her from behind. Julie is first to see Oik –

Julie: Jesus!

Stormboy turns to see the spectre of Oik staring.

Oik: What are you doing?

Stormboy disengages. As Stormboy comes towards him, hurriedly doing himself up, Oik retreats.

Stormboy: What's happened?

Oik: What the fuck are you doing? With her!

The door to the TV room flies open and Terry and Cat spill out –

Terry: Hammers one-up! Yee-EESSSSS!!

– followed by Davey.

Davey: Just fetch us a bevvy and shut up.

Oik: (*still absolutely intent on Stormboy*) Are you fucking mad?

As this draws the others' attention to them –

Cat: Boy, you should have seen –

She gasps as Oik turns towards them, staggering a few steps away from Stormboy.

Terry: Bloody hell . . .

Stormboy: Oik –

Oik: Don't you talk to me! Don't you fucking . . .

He looks like he's about to cry – but kicks out at chairs and stools.

Davey: Oy!

Caught between the two groups – Cat, Terry and Davey on one side, Stormboy on the other – Oik stumbles back against the bar, and pulls out the knife.

Oik: Nobody touch me!

Julie emerges from the toilet, coat pulled round her. Terry steps quietly forward to Oik.

Terry: You need to get that seen to, son. Down at A & E.

Oik slowly focuses on Terry.

Car's outside – I'll take you.

Oik: They were fucking.

He nods in the direction of Stormboy and, further back, Julie.

She was fucking him.

Terry looks across at Julie. She looks back.

The stools Oik is propped against give way and with a crash and a clatter they and Oik hit the floor.

END OF ACT 1

ACT 2

Later. Cat is outside on the landing. She screams at Stormboy –

Cat: Just FUCK OFF!

Stormboy retreats inside. Cat turns to moodily staring out and drinking heavily from the cider bottle. The sound of the match comes from the TV room where Davey is the only one still watching.

Davey: (*off*) What yer doin' Ref?

Stormboy slumps on a stool and presses his palms to his eyes. In the background there's a sound – the snap of a bag being inflated, and rasping breathing. It's repeated. Stormboy takes his hands away from his face. It's a sound he recognises. He ducks behind the bar and hauls Oik out of the cupboard –

Oik: Hey – !

Stormboy snatches the plastic bag Oik is sniffing from.

Stormboy: What's this?

Oik shows him what he's got in his other hand.

Oik: Lighter fluid. A whole tin of it just going to waste.

Stormboy grabs the lighter fluid and shoves it back on a shelf in the cupboard, before bundling Oik into the centre of the room. Stormboy looks like he could attack Oik but, not able to express his frustration any other way, he shakes him. And shakes him and shakes him and shakes him. Oik's response is to go limp as he's thrown about like a doll. He starts to cough. Stormboy stops, lets go of him. Oik is wracked by coughing and wheezing.

Stormboy: Where is it?

Oik can't answer – but starts to go through his pockets. Stormboy becomes more concerned at his breathlessness.

Did you bring it?

Oik is slumped on the floor, gasping. Stormboy takes over the search and finds the asthma inhaler in one of Oik's pockets. Oik gives himself a squirt. Stormboy relaxes, sitting on the floor with his back against the bar.

Stormboy: What'd ya tell him for?

Oik: Bitch.

He slips his inhaler back in his pocket and drags himself over beside Stormboy.

I told you that's all they think about. Dirty old —

Stormboy: Get a girlfriend. Get someone else to pull it for a change.

Oik: Fuck you.

Pause.

Stormboy: You're a lunatic.

Oik starts singing the Sid Vicious version of 'My Way'.

Who stomped you?

Oik keeps singing.

So you found the knife. What'd you do — go through every bin? Did you see any cops?

Oik: (*shakes his head*) Just those cunts from Lower Hutt.

Stormboy: The Boots?

Oik: Bitches who hang round with them. Chased me. Bit upset about their mate.

Stormboy: What'd they say about him?

Oik: I slipped over. They were straight in — kicked me in the head. But I came up with the knife, didn't I? Then it was my turn to play chasey.

Stormboy: Did they say he was . . .[dead]

Oik looks at him, seeing his fear.

Oik: Up the hospital.

Stormboy: Hospital?

Oik: (*shrugs*) Whistling out his chest, that's all. He won't come in here again in a hurry.

> *Stormboy takes a breath, lets it out, eyes closed.*

Stormboy: Shit.

> *He lets go of the tension he has been holding.*

Shit . . .

> *Stormboy opens his eyes.*

Beaten up by girls, eh?

Oik: I slipped!

Stormboy: Hefty girls, some of them.

Oik: Should've seen them running – bloody herd of elephants – with me trying to poke my knife up their bums.

(*looks round*) Where is it anyway?

Stormboy: Herd of elephants – that's seen a mouse.

> *He snorts.*

Oik: Get fucked.

Stormboy: The hospital – they said that?

Oik: What I said, isn't it?

> *Stormboy is almost tripping on the relief. Oik regards him.*

D'you know how stupid you looked? Pants round your ankles, your big white hairy bum –

Stormboy: I'd look a lot more stupid without my head – which I thought Terry was going to take off for me.

(*looks in direction of TV room*) Or him.

Oik: (*scathing*) And with her –

Stormboy: She's alright.

Oik: What kind of noise does she make? Like a washing machine?

             He makes a grotesque chugging sucking noise.

             Did that turn you on?

Stormboy: Knock it off.

             Oik exaggerates the noise, adding farting sounds.

             I said –

Oik: That's what sex is! That's all it is! Then you die!

Stormboy: What's your problem?

             And Oik has got a problem – something, the only thing, he's passionate about – something on a grand scale which he struggles frustratedly to articulate.

Oik: They're – not . . . us! They're – old! Shit! We don't . . . we're . . . you know! You know! You – !

             Unable to get there – without the words – he starts banging the back of his head against the side of the bar, progressively harder. Stormboy moves to stop him, has to grab his head to force him to a halt.

Stormboy: Hey! Hey, hey, hey . . .

             Oik sings the last line of 'My Way' – loud. Davey shouts from the TV room –

Davey: (*off*) Fuck up!

             Stormboy has his hand on the back of Oik's neck.

Oik: He knew.

Stormboy: Sid?

Oik: When he'd see a hippie he'd just walk up, smack 'em in the face and shout 'Remember the Summer of Love?' He knew what he was kicking against. He was for real. And he proved it.

Stormboy: Did he?

Oik: He didn't give a fuck what anyone else thought. It was his life. And when he'd had enough he just checked out.

Stormboy decides to commit heresy.

Stormboy: Maybe he was just scared.

Oik: Scared?

Stormboy: Of this whole thing he started. Getting stuck in it.

Oik: He wasn't scared of anything! He gave the finger to the world!

Stormboy: Maybe he couldn't see any way out – of what everyone wanted him to be.

Oik sings another line of 'My Way' loudly, to drown Stormboy out.

Davey: (*off*) Fuck up, before I come out there and thump you!

Stormboy: (*like a kid*) He started it!

Oik cuffs at him. Stormboy cuffs back. They flail at each other like kids squabbling. Stormboy grins.

You heard what Dad said.

Oik looks at him, grins too. Pause.

Oik: I didn't start it. With that boot boy. He was giving me shit – about the lamb.

Not a subject Stormboy wants to discuss.

Nobody'll talk to me. They've all heard about it. Thanks to her.

Stormboy: What'd you expect?

Oik: I don't give a fuck.

Stormboy: Then don't talk about it.

Silence.

Oik: Do you think about it?

        Stormboy shakes his head.

        I think about it.

Stormboy: Then why'd you do it?

Oik: It was him or me.

Stormboy: A lamb?

Oik: (*serious*) It was. Him or me. Story of Isaac.

Stormboy: Eh?

Oik: Isaac and Abraham.

        Stormboy looks at him.

Stormboy: (*sings quietly*) Rock my soul in the bosom of Abraham
Rock my soul in the bosom of Abraham Gonna rock my
soul in de bosom of Abraham –

        Oik joins in, waving his hands black-and-white minstrel style –

Stormboy/Oik: Oh – rock my soul!

        Pause.

Stormboy: I ever tell you about when I saw Bob Marley on *Ready
To Roll*?

Oik: Bob Marley?

        *Stormboy sings a snatch of 'Lively Up Yourself'. Oik doesn't
believe him.*

        Piss off.

Stormboy: This was a year before the Pistols. First reggae I'd ever
heard. I kinda sat up. You know, it wasn't Roxy Music – or
Boz Scaggs. Or Pink Floyd that my brother was thrashing –
'Shine On You Crazy Diamond' and all that shit. I took the
train all the way into town to check that Marley record out.

Oik: Fuckin' bong-head music?

Stormboy sings the opening of 'Three O'clock Road-Block'.

Stormboy: Shoulda heard my brother when I brought it home. 'What's this spook shit?' All of a sudden I had something. Something I liked that made me different. Just one problem. I wasn't black. I was never going to be black – no matter how much I waxed my hair into dreadlocks, or smoked ganga. I wasn't living in funky Kingston town – I was living in Grenada. The arse-end of Tawa. The last suburb God made.

Oik: So?

Stormboy: So I had to wait. Another year. For a –

He sings 'White Riot'. Oik joins in happily.

The bathroom door opens and Julie comes out. Her face – underneath a thin layer of make-up – shows she has been crying. She looks at Stormboy and Oik – Oik looks away pointedly. Julie heads behind the bar, lights a cigarette, runs water into the sink and starts to wash up glasses and ashtrays.

Where did Terry go?

Julie shrugs.

Oik: (*sniffs*) You smell something?

Stormboy: If I was him – I'd be pretty wild . . .

Julie: But you ain't him, are you? My advice – keep it that way.

Oik: Didn't think those fishing boats were so close.

Stormboy: Shut it.

(*to Julie*) How do you mean?

Julie: Don't marry someone like me for a kick-off.

Oik: Not fresh, that's for sure.

Julie: What's he on about?

Stormboy: Nothing.

Oik: Stinking rotten old fish, that's what I smell!

Julie snatches up an ashtray like she's going to throw it.

Julie: Get him out of my sight. Or I swear I'll do for him.

Stormboy looks caught.

Stormboy: We'd better go.

Oik: 'Bout fucking time.

Oik scrambles to his feet, and heads for the door. Stormboy hesitates – then follows. Julie watches.

Julie: Cops are still looking for you aren't they?

Stormboy shrugs.

Here –

Julie takes a key from a hook inside the cupboard. She unlocks the door backstage right and pulls it open. It's stiff on its hinges, not much used.

You can go down in the Rowing Club. Long as you leave the lights off and keep out of sight.

Stormboy: Thanks.

Julie: Just mind him.

She picks up a tea-towel behind the bar and starts drying.

Oik: I'm not going down there.

Stormboy: Yes you are.

Oik: It's dark, and cold –

Stormboy: Just get down there.

He pushes Oik towards the doorway. As Oik passes the end of the bar he palms Julie's lighter from beside her cigarettes, before exiting. Stormboy has turned to Julie.

Stormboy: He's not dead. The boot boy – at the party. He's at the hospital. Going to be alright.

Julie: Good. That's good.

Stormboy: I really thought . . . [I'd killed him]

Julie: You'll probably be boasting about it tomorrow.

She turns away, busying herself with the drying. Stormboy lingers, a little awkward.

Stormboy: It was my fault. Before.

Julie: You can thank Mouth Almighty down there for that.

Stormboy: I mean – my fault for starting it.

She regards him evenly.

Julie: Do that often, do you? Turn women into jelly, get them melting into puddles at your feet with no will of their own?

Stormboy: No –

Julie: No – and you didn't do it to me neither. I'm not one of your lame ducks. I'll take the blame for what I do myself, thank you very much.

Stormboy: Feel like I should be here when Terry comes back.

Julie: If he comes back.

Stormboy: You're waiting for him, aren't you?

Julie: I got no choice. He took the car.

Stormboy: Catch a taxi.

Julie: I need the car. I need what's in the car.

(*mutters*) Suitcase, passport . . .

Stormboy: Eh?

Julie: My passport. In the boot of the car.

Stormboy stares at her.

Julie: Where do you think I was when that phone rang, eh? Packing.

(*pained at how close she was to getting away*) I was zipping up my bloody suitcase. All set. Airline tickets – the lot. This? My lovely nightie? I had to get undressed again – throw this on to come down here. Right, I think. Come by, drop the telly – and gone. No messing.

(*laughs sickly*) No messing!

(*pulls herself up*) But that's me all over. I think things is bad enough – but when it comes to it, I've got to do something to make it so bloody atrocious that it gets me off my chuff and through the door.

(*takes a breath*) Well, we're there now. Bloody brilliant, Jools . . . surpassed yourself.

Stormboy: You're just going to walk out? Go back to London?

Julie: You don't say a word, you understand? Just keep your head down –

Stormboy: And you're not going to say anything to Terry?

Julie has somehow expected Stormboy to be on her side.

Julie: What's it to you – actually?

Stormboy: I like him.

Julie: You what?

(*gazes at him*) You like him. All boys together. Well, I love him. Alright?

(*dismissive*) What would you know about it? What would you know about anything?

(*ending the conversation*) – Here.

She slaps down on the bar what she has been rubbing with the tea-towel. Oik's knife. Stormboy reaches for it – but Julie grabs him by the wrist.

Julie: Someone must've put it in the washing-up.

She leans across the bar.

Looks like God's decided to give you a chance. If you get out of this – use your loaf from here on.

Davey emerges from the TV room. He looks at Julie witheringly.

Davey: Still not got enough?

Julie: You just shut yer hole, Davey.

Davey: Should've shut yours 'n' all.

Stormboy starts to rouse himself at this – but Julie gestures him back.

Julie: Oy!

(*less peremptory*) Go see if your mate's alright. He's probably drilling holes in their boats.

Stormboy stares at her.

Go on.

He goes.

Davey: What you doing letting them down there?

Julie: So I don't murder that little mongrel up here.

Davey looks at her, shakes his head.

Davey: You really know how to make an evening.

Julie: Disgusted by me, are you?

Davey: I'm on my own in there.

Julie: Face it, Davey – you're on your own everywhere.

Davey: I know I can't talk –

Julie: Glad to hear it.

Davey: He's a kid!

Julie: Is he? Didn't feel like it in there.

Davey: You take the cake, you do.

Julie: Where's all the outrage coming from, Davey? Me betraying your best mate – my husband – or just that you can't get your head round the fact that it wasn't you?

Davey: Bloody walking bottlebrush – what's he got?

Julie: Nothing out the ordinary. Only what you've all got.

Davey: Eh?

Julie: Sperm.

Davey: You're twisted, you are. I don't even know what the fuck you're on about.

Julie: No change there then. You never did have any idea, did you Davey?

Davey: (*turning to go*) I give up –

Julie: What I'm on about? What I'm all over the bleeding shop about! Babies as a matter of fact.

Davey: Babies? You 'n' Terry don't want kids. You said so often enough – the pair of you.

Julie: There might be a valuable lesson for you here, Davey – if you concentrate hard enough.

Davey: I'm going back to the match.

          He turns – but before he can reach the door –

Julie: People don't always tell the truth!

          He stops, turns to look at her.

Davey: You trying to – [tell me]? You said you were on the pill.

Julie: I just didn't say what pill.

          She darts a defiant look at him.

          I was on the fertility pill.

Davey is stunned.

Davey: You evil bitch.

Julie: That's right …

Julie seems to shrink as –

Davey: You would've had a kid – my kid – !

Julie: Didn't work. Nothing works.

Davey: – and pretended to Terry … Bring it up – with him not knowing? Make a bloody idiot out of him?

Julie: He's not the idiot.

Davey: Somebody needs to see to you.

    (strides across to her) If he's too soft to do it – !

Julie: I am! I'm the idiot!

She holds his stare. Davey lowers his hand.

Davey: You're not worth it.

Julie: Davey …

Davey: I wouldn't piss on you if you were drowning.

Julie: He wouldn't take a test. He wouldn't even have a test. To find out.

Davey: *(moving away)* Don't tell me, I don't wanna know.

Julie: *(grabs him)* Your great mate Terry – always a smile, slap on the back –

Davey: *(trying to push her away)* I said I ain't interested –

Julie: He wouldn't do that for me – for his wife!

Davey: *(shakes her)* D'ya hear me! What's wrong with you?

Julie spreads her arms.

Julie: I just need to be rooted. That's what they say here, innit? I'm desperate for a root.

Davey: (*stares at her*) Yer bleedin' psycho, is what you are.

He turns and walks back into the other room. Julie slumps back down at the bar, takes out a cigarette but can't find her lighter. She scrabbles about distractedly, finds some matches and shakily lights the cigarette.

Terry comes up the outside stairs. Seeing Cat, he stops.

Terry: Hey up.

Cat doesn't turn or reply. Terry looks at the door to inside, then joins Cat at the railing, staring out into the night. Cat drinks.

Still chugging that down – you must have intestines of steel.

Cat shrugs, affecting not caring about anything.

I know – it feels like the worst thing in the world right now –

Cat: What d'you know about it.

Terry: Only that it was my wife with your boyfriend.

Cat looks at him.

Cat: Sorry.

Terry: I'm sorry 'n' all. It shouldn't happen to anyone, let alone a nice kid like you.

Cat: I'm not a kid.

Terry: A charming young lady like yourself.

Cat looks at him a moment.

Cat: Don't feel very charming. If I was charming –

On the brink of crying, she tries to finish, gesturing inside –

– he wouldn't – he wouldn't . . .

Terry: Hey . . .

He puts a hand on her shoulder.

Terry: Lads do stupid things. They all do. Then they turn round and say 'What the hell did I do that stupid thing for?'

Cat: Did you?

Terry: Stupid does not even begin to describe some of the things I did.

Cat: Like marrying her?

Terry stiffens – but lets it go.

Terry: How's our boy Oik?

Cat: Don't know, couldn't care.

Terry: Looked nasty.

Cat: He's always fighting, causing trouble, counting on Boy to get him out. After what he did to that lamb . . .

Terry: How's that?

Cat: Boy told me not to talk about it. But –

(raises her voice to carry inside) – he can get fucked!

Everyone knows anyway.

She looks at Terry.

We went up to this party in Levin. Outside Levin. They had this lamb out the back – you know, on a chain with a little house and everything. Everyone was playing with it and giving it drinks, it was so cute. Then later on we heard this – screaming. And Oik had poured something on it – and set it alight.

Terry: Set it – ? Never.

Cat: He set it on fire. A lamb. Someone threw their coat over it – but it was so hurt – they had to cut its throat. I thought I was going to vomit.

Terry: Had to've been an accident. He's a bit of an idiot at times, but –

Cat: He just stood there, watching it. Boy had to get us out of there fast. Just like tonight.

Terry absorbs this.

He hasn't got any friends left – except for Boy. He's lied to everyone. He'll tell you anything just to upset you. Or because he thinks it's what Boy wants to hear. And he hates me.

Terry: Fancies you for himself, more like.

Cat: No one wants to be round Boy anymore because he's always there. I'm the only one. And then he just goes and . . .

(*crying*) He wouldn't even do it with me. Before. I wanted to. I'm his girlfriend . . .

Terry: There you go, then. You didn't say 'was his girlfriend'. That's got to be a good sign. Eh?

She looks at him, sniffing.

Cat: What are you going to do? You going to leave her? Get a divorce?

Terry is almost amused – but tries not to show it.

Terry: What are you going to do?

Cat doesn't have an answer to that.

Maybe they've both learned their lesson, eh?

Cat: She's done it before.

Terry glances at her sharply.

Terry: Who told you that?

Cat: Nobody.

Terry: Don't be too quick to judge, love.

Cat: Why do you let her?

Terry: It's not a case of 'letting' anyone.

Cat: Why stay with her then?

Terry looks at her.

Terry: Nothing that would make any sense to you.

He straightens up, ready to go inside. Cat wants the company.

Cat: What was it about her – made you want to get married?

Terry: That's all an age ago, girl. Prehistoric.

Cat: Tell me.

Terry considers.

Terry: Well – she was the prettiest girl I'd ever seen. With the exception of Marianne Faithfull. And she was taken.

Cat: Was that all?

Terry: She was – game. Whatever I thought of, she'd be right there. Any lunatic thing. She had more nerve than anyone I ever saw.

He turns to Cat.

You know, on this scooter I had – her on the back – I put it under a bus once. Missed the brake, laid it over, we slid right under this Number 48 to Waterloo Bridge. Well she did – and the bike did – I smacked up against the side. I was beside myself, couldn't see her under there for the scooter jammed in the way. Broken mirror glass everywhere. Thought I'd killed her. I was shouting, 'Julie! Julie!' Then her voice comes out from underneath. 'Sod off, Terry – I'm catching the bus home.'

He gazes out.

Cat: If I was married to you, I wouldn't . . . I'd be faithful.

Terry: Even Marianne wasn't always faithful.

Cat: I would be. If I was – you know – your age.

Terry has to smile.

Terry: Well, that's the nicest thing anyone's said to me tonight.

There's a warm moment – which Terry ends.

Coming inside?

Cat shakes her head.

Want me to send him out?

Cat hesitates.

You stay here. I'll talk to him.

Terry opens the door and goes in, closing it behind him. Cat sags down into sitting position – soon she will curl up on her side. Julie doesn't turn round as Terry comes in. He looks at her.

What's the score?

Julie glances at him, snorts. Terry moves round to behind the bar, gets himself a beer out of the cupboard. With a label on it.

Julie: 'Harrison'.

Terry: I'll pay it back.

Julie: And if you forget to pay it back, Terry?

Terry: Fuck 'em.

Julie: That's my boy.

They sit for a moment.

I'm tired, Terry.

He regards her steadily.

I'd like to go home. Have you got the keys?

Terry: Course I've got the keys. I've just got out the car, haven't I?

Julie: Could I have them? Can I go home?

Terry: I need to stay here, see everything's locked up after the match. We had a break-in . . .

Julie: Terry, I know we need to talk. Let's do it tomorrow, eh? When I can think straight.

Terry: I'll call you a cab.

Julie: Davey can drop you home. Just give me the keys.

Terry: I want the car.

Julie looks at him, shrugs.

Julie: I need to get something out.

Terry: What?

Julie: Tampons.

Terry: You've got tampons in the car?

Julie: I'm a woman, Terry. I've got tampons everywhere.

Terry: (*getting up*) I'll come down and unlock it.

Julie blocks him.

Julie: What's wrong with you?

Terry: My wife's fucking other blokes. Apart from that I'm a bobby dazzler.

Julie absorbs this, sits down again.

Julie: What d'you want me to say? 'Sorry'? That's going to go a long way isn't it?

Terry: Terry and Julie.

Julie hangs her head.

Julie: Oh, for fuck's sake . . .

Terry: Terry and Julie.

Julie: Did you ever think – just one time while you were listening to that song – what happened to Terry and Julie when they grew up?

Terry: Yeah. I did.

Julie: And where are they now, Terry? Did they emigrate?

Terry: They stayed together.

Julie looks at him.

Julie: Just the two of them?

Terry: Two – four – six – eight – they stayed together!

She can't meet his eye.

Julie: Boy and his mate are downstairs. If the cops turn up, you ain't seen them.

Terry: What's doing?

Julie: Just a fight. That little shit stirring it.

She puts her hand on his.

Terry, I'm whacked. Out on my feet. I need to go home.

Terry: Home?

Julie: For God's sake – you've heard of the concept – four walls, a roof over your head!

Terry looks at her. He takes the car keys out, hands them to her.

Terry: You get yourself in the warm.

She stands.

Julie: See you then.

Terry: See you.

Julie moves to give him a kiss – but Terry puts his hand up to stop her. She accepts this – turns and goes. On the landing she finds Cat asleep. She thinks of calling Terry – but flags it, steps over Cat and goes down the stairs. Terry removes Julie's passport from the back pocket of his trousers, taps it against his hand, considering – then puts it into the inside pocket of his jacket, zipping it in. He sits at the bar. From the TV room comes the sound of the end of the match – and of Davey swearing.

Davey: (*off*) Bollocks! Bloody buggery bollocks . . . !

Davey comes out of the TV room. He stops, seeing Terry. Terry doesn't acknowledge him.

Julie gone?

No answer. Davey takes refuge in football talk.

You didn't miss much. West Ham – one-nil. Never changed from quarter-time. Arsenal were a waste of bloody space.

Terry doesn't respond. Davey looks round uncomfortably.

Reckon I'll get off now. Am I giving you a lift?

Terry: I'll hang on here. Said I'd have a word to Boy.

As Terry gets off the stool, heading for the door down to the rowing club –

Davey: Need me to watch your back?

Terry: Eh?

Davey: That toe-rag's got it coming and no mistake. After what you've done for him, and the dirty little fucker goes and –

Terry swings on Davey, dangerous.

Terry: Toe-rag, is he? Dirty little fucker? For having it away with my wife?

Davey: Only saying . . .

Terry: I wouldn't if I was you, Davey. I wouldn't even open my big fat gob.

Terry turns – and disappears down the stairs.

Davey: Well that's just frigging charming.

The room is empty. Davey looks glumly around. He crosses to put on his coat, take his peaked cap from its peg . . . Meanwhile, as the discomfort of the buckled wet wood underneath her seeps in, Cat has twisted and rolled to where first an arm has lolled out into space, then her head and upper body, to the point where she is perilously close to toppling off the landing. She knocks over the almost-empty cider bottle, it rumbles across the wood and over the edge. We hear it splash twenty feet below.

Davey crosses the room and flings open the door – hard against Cat, pushing her over the edge, the top half of her body swinging out over the black drop. Only the fact that her legs and cherry docs are pinned by the door against one of the shaky uprights stops her from sliding off. Looking down and spotting Cat's legs and boots, all that is visible of her, Davey stops dead.

Davey: Jesus!

On reflex, Davey releases pressure on the door and straightaway Cat's docs slide towards the edge with the weight of her body. Davey jams himself against the door to wedge the boots. He looks round for help –

Terry – !

– but there is none. Keeping his weight against the door, he shuffles out to where he can grab Cat's ankles, then carefully stretch down to grasp the waistband of her skirt or studded belt. He takes a breath, then, releasing his shoulder from against the door, he lets it swing back and hauls Cat up. She is blissfully unaware of her close call.

What're you playing at, girl? You stupid . . . !

Cat just mumbles and turns into a foetal position on her side, knees drawn up.

You'll die of exposure out here. Come on –

He scoops her up and carries her inside. As he looks for somewhere to put her down – Oik comes quietly up from downstairs, lighting his way with Julie's lighter. Seeing Davey, he stops.

Oik: You dirty old cunt.

Davey spins round.

Get your fucking hands off her.

Davey: Keep your hair on. She's out to it.

He sets her gently down in recovery position. She groans and goes to turn over. Davey stops her.

Keep still, girl.

Oik: Get your hands off!

He jumps across and pushes Davey away. Davey grabs him by the front of his clothes and pulls him up.

Davey: Time you were leaving.

Oik, with deliberation, spits right in Davey's face. Davey hurls him away.

I'll kill you!

As Davey advances, Oik throws a stool at him and dodges behind the bar. Davey pursues him – but then stops and backs up.

Oik: You fuck off.

Oik has found the knife and, holding it in front of him, emerges from behind the bar.

You keep away from me. Keep away from her! Just fuck off!

Davey picks up a stool and holds it sideways.

Davey: What're you going to do with that, sunshine? Cut me?

Oik: I already stabbed a guy tonight.

Davey: You?

Oik: Killed the fucker. You come near me and you'll get the same.

Davey uses the stool to crowd Oik back until he's against the bar.

Davey: You know what? If you managed to do that without fucking it up, I'd be the first to shake you by the hand.

On 'hand' he grasps Oik's wrist. The knife is held up like Excalibur between them. Davey pushes the stool against Oik and slowly applies his full force to crush him against the bar. Oik grimaces in pain and struggles to breathe. Davey lets the stool fall, spins Oik round and jerks his arm up savagely behind his back until he drops the knife. Davey lifts Oik clear of the bar and smashes his head into it face first. Davey is struggling to control his anger –

Davey: Pull a knife on me, you little shit!

He knees Oik in the back. Oik screams. Davey hauls him away from the bar –

Right. Couldn't be better. Couldn't be better.

Looking round he sees the cupboard and drags Oik towards it. He has his hand around Oik's face – he suddenly jerks it away.

Fuckin' bite me!

He shoves Oik into the cupboard. When Oik realises what is happening, he tries to cling to the doorway but Davey bashes his fingers till he can push him in and slam the door. He turns the key in the lock just as Oik throws himself against the door. As Davey turns away to the phone –

Miserable little rat –

– Stormboy comes up from downstairs. Oik continues to crash against the door of the cupboard.

Stormboy: What's going on?

Davey glances at him, then pulls the key out of the lock.

Davey: Your mate. He went for me – with that.

He points to the knife still lying on the floor.

Stormboy: Let him out.

Davey: Not fucking likely. That's assault with an offensive weapon, that is.

A crashing and smashing comes from the cupboard as Oik pulls the contents of the shelves down.

Davey: Go ahead – wreck the bloody place – see if I care!

Stormboy: Let him out. He's claustrophobic.

Davey: I don't care if he's fuckin' hydrophobic. The cops can deal to him.

Davey picks up the phone and dials.

Stormboy: Let him out! NOW!

Oik hears Stormboy's voice and pummels on the door –

Oik: Boy? Boy!

Davey regards Stormboy steadily.

Davey: You can go with him. All the same to me.

Waiting for the phone to be answered, Davey keeps an eye on Stormboy who moves to the cupboard door, pulling on it.

Stormboy: Oik!

Oik: Get me out!

Stormboy smashes angrily at the door but it doesn't budge.

Davey: (*on the phone, with a noticeably more kiwi accent*) Who's that? Alan – Dave Moore here. Got a pick-up for you, mate. Assault with a weapon. Club down on the wharf – boatshed. That's the one.

He hangs up. Stormboy turns to him grimly.

Stormboy: Gimme the key.

As he speaks, Davey reaches into his coat pocket –

Davey: Couldn't do that. I'd look a right prat if the boys arrive and I tell them I let a couple of weedy punks get the better of me.

Stormboy: (*stepping forward*) Give it to me!

Davey holds up the key.

Davey: Come and get it.

Stormboy goes for the key. Davey pulls the truncheon from his coat pocket and batons Stormboy across the head, knocking him back and onto the floor.

Davey: Come on ...

Blood is running from Stormboy's hairline. He sees the knife and goes for it – but Davey steps on it.

Couldn't be better.

Julie comes quickly back up the stairs.

Julie: Terry!

(*bursting in*) Where's – ?

She stops, taking in the scene.

What's this?

Davey: None of yours.

Oik pounds on the door –

Oik: BOY!

With his foot, Davey shoves the knife along the floor to Stormboy.

Davey: All yours, cock.

Stormboy looks at it.

Come on now – be a hero – rescue your mate.

As Stormboy moves to grasp the knife –

Julie: No!

She grabs Stormboy from behind and drags him back, hoisting him to his feet.

Leave it. Get out of here.

As she moves round to face Stormboy, Davey holds the key up and goads over Julie's shoulder –

Davey: Come on, punk boy – show us what you got.

Julie: (*pushing Stormboy back*) Get out.

Davey: You thin streak of piss.

Terry appears at the door from downstairs, takes one look and knocks the key flying from Davey's hand –

Hey – !

– then head-butts him. Davey goes down like a sack of spuds. Terry kicks him – and keeps kicking him – Davey rolling over and over trying to avoid the kicking until he fetches up against the wall where Terry keeps battering him. Julie has pushed Stormboy out onto the landing.

Stormboy: He's called the cops.

Julie: Then go.

Stormboy: Oik –

Julie: He'll be alright! GO!

She shoves him towards the stairs. With a backward glance, Stormboy runs out.

Terry: You were meant to be my mate!

He gives Davey a last kick. Davey groans.

I should've been able to trust you. With my wife. My wife!

Terry is almost in tears.

Julie: (*gently*) Terry . . .

Terry looks at her, then staggers to a barstool.

Oik: Boy! BOY!

Julie moves to the cupboard door.

Julie: He's gone.

A startled beat, then –

Oik: You're lying.

Julie: He's gone. He's got himself to think about.

Oik: (*throwing himself against the door*) You're lying! Let me out of
               here, you cunts! LET ME OUT!

Julie: You can stay put, you evil little bastard. You've caused enough
               trouble.

               Davey is stirring, groaning. Julie crosses to help him up.

               You alright?

               *Davey pushes her hand away. He looks at Terry, then staggers past
               him to the door and exits down the stairs. Oik starts to sing the Sid
               Vicious version of 'My Way' which grows underneath what follows.*

Terry: You'd better get off. Before the cops get here.

               She looks at him. He takes her passport out, puts it on the bar.

               Went home. Saw your clothes were gone. Found your
               suitcase in the car boot.

Julie: It seemed easier – to just go.

               Terry nods.

               Every time we talk about it . . .

Terry: I'll pick the car up from the airport.

Julie: If you hadn't rung –

Terry: Then just go. Now. Before the boys in blue want to be
               standing round taking down names and addresses.

               *Julie hesitates, looks like she's going to say something, then reaches
               out and picks up the passport. Terry doesn't look at her. She crosses
               to the door.*

               Put a dress on before Heathrow.

               *Julie glances back with a pained smile. Oik's performance of 'My
               Way' reaches its crescendo –*

There's an audible 'whoomph' from inside the cupboard, and a glow of light around the cracks of the door. Oik screams. Followed by more screams, and crashing as Oik lunges frantically back and forth inside the cupboard. Terry leaps round the bar to yank at the door –

Julie: The key, Terry! The key!

She searches desperately for it on the floor where it was knocked from Davey's hand. She can't find it. Oik's screams are blood-curdling, smoke starts to seep around the door-frame. Cat stirs, and wakes as Terry smashes his shoulder against the door – it doesn't move. Again. Nothing.

Terry: The key!

Julie: I can't find it! Oh Jesus, Terry, I can't find it!

Terry picks up a stool and batters at the door. Suddenly Julie spots the key and snatches it up –

Terry!

He grabs the key, fumbles it urgently into the lock and yanks the door open. Flame bursts out, and billowing black smoke, driving Terry back. Cat has staggered up, groggy, in time to see into the cupboard as the door bursts open. She screams. Blackout.

Music: 'My Way'. Sirens.

Lights up slowly on the stairs. The inside of the club remains shrouded in darkness and smoke – it has been wrecked by the fire. The sound of water dripping in its sodden interior. It is a few hours later, just before dawn. Julie is sitting hunched near the top of the stairs, face tucked into her knees – tired, grimy and cold.

Stormboy comes quietly up the stairs. He looks for a moment over Julie to the slightly open door, smoke escaping.

Stormboy: He did this, didn't he?

Julie looks up. She has been close to an exhausted sleep.

Stormboy: I saw it. All the fire engines and everything.

> *Julie bites her lip.*

Sorry.

Julie: (*almost crying*) It shouldn't be you who's sorry –

Stormboy: The club –

Julie: That doesn't matter.

> *Julie takes his wrist, pulls him down beside her.*

Stormboy: Did they get him? I bet he didn't even have the sense to run away.

> *Julie is starting to suspect Stormboy doesn't understand.*

Julie: Boy . . .

Stormboy: What? Where is he?

> *Julie glances up at the door. Confused, Stormboy jumps up as if he's going to look inside.*

Julie: It's us who should be sorry.

> *Stormboy stares at her, then towards the smoking interior.*

Stormboy: You left him there? You left him locked in?

Julie: I didn't know he'd do that.

Stormboy: You told me it'd be alright. You told me to go.

> *Julie nods miserably. Stormboy suddenly jerks her to her feet angrily.*

You told me!

Terry: Hoy –

> *Terry enters to stand a few steps down.*

Hands off.

> *Stormboy lets go of Julie. Terry moves to gather her in.*

Stormboy: He's dead?

Terry: (*tight*) Yeah.

Stormboy: You – [cunts!]

Terry: None o'that.

Stormboy: You killed him! You locked him up – !

Terry: We didn't soak him with lighter fluid and set him alight. He did that himself. To hisself.

(*shakes his head*) What he's done to his parents –

Stormboy: His parents! They don't give a fuck!

Terry: Don't be stupid!

Stormboy: Nobody does!

Terry: That's baby talk! That's what killed him!

Stormboy: You thought he was joking. To you it was all a laugh. Something we'd grow out of. Well he's not going to grow out of it, is he?

Terry: And that's something to be proud of?

Stormboy: Were his boots burnt?

Terry: Were what?

Stormboy: His boots!

Julie: Boy . . .

Stormboy shies away as she goes to touch him. Davey comes up the stairs and stops. Bruises are coming up round his eyes from the head-butt, the fingers of one hand are splinted and in a sling. He doesn't look at Stormboy.

Davey: The Fire boys want to seal the building. You'll have to go through them to get anything out.

Terry: Right.

Davey hesitates, aware he's not that popular, wanting to justify himself.

Davey: What he was raving about – stabbing someone . . . turns out it wasn't bullshit. Mate of mine on the Force says they've been looking for him all night. That was why he did it. Scared of going down for it – couldn't face it.

Julie glances at Stormboy.

Julie: Alright then. That's best for everyone, isn't it?

Davey looks at Julie, accepts that. But as he turns away –

Stormboy: That's crap.

They look at him.

He wasn't scared. He wasn't scared of anything.

Davey: I'd called the police. He knew he was going to get done. Big time.

Stormboy: He wasn't going to get shit. He didn't stab that guy.

Davey: Eh?

Julie: Boy –

Stormboy: I did. I stabbed him. Oik didn't have nothing to do with it.

Terry: What're you doing?

Davey: This isn't some sort of game. If what you're saying is right –

Terry: Leave it, Davey. It makes no difference now. Forget he said it.

Stormboy: (*to Davey*) You heard me. Oik wasn't scared!

Julie: Davey –

Stormboy: You fuckin' keep out of it!

Terry: We're trying to help you!

Davey: This is serious, this is. I can't just ignore it like it was a parking ticket!

Terry: There's been enough –

Stormboy: It was his life. And when he'd had enough he just checked out. He was for real.

Terry: You want to be like him? Throw everything away – when there's no point?

Stormboy: There is no point! And no future!

(jabs his fist in the air) Anarchy!

Terry: *(raising his fist)* D'you want me to knock some sense into you?

Stormboy: *(in Terry's face, grappling for the words like Oik earlier)* You! And her! I don't want nothing – nothing from you! You don't know . . . us. You don't know! So just fuck off! FUCK OFF!

Terry stares at him. Steps back. Defiant, Stormboy faces Davey.

I stabbed him. Fuckin' boot boy. He was asking for it.

Davey is almost gentle.

Davey: There was still a D.I. over by the gate a minute ago. I'll take you over – you can tell him yourself.

Stormboy shrugs, comes down a few stairs, glances at the burnt-out club.

Stormboy: I wanna be out for Oik's funeral. Salute the fallen.

Davey: I wouldn't count on that.

Stormboy: Assault. They'll give me bail.

Davey: Assault?

Stormboy stops, looks at him.

Stormboy: The guy's ok – he's up the hospital . . .

Davey: Cop talking to me said it was straight through the heart. Died before the ambulance got there.

Stormboy: But Oik . . . he told me . . .

He realises. They realise. Julie crumples.

Julie: Oh, Jesus.

Davey: What did you think I was talking about? They've got a murder inquiry underway.

Terry: (*to Stormboy*) You bloody . . . stupid . . .

Davey: You're in the First Division now, sunshine. I can't keep a lid on this.

              Stormboy casts a lost glance up at Terry – but both know it's too late.

Terry: (*hardens*) Go on then.

              Davey takes Stormboy's elbow gently.

Davey: Come on, son. No point delaying.

              They walk down the stairs. Just before they disappear, Stormboy turns to look up towards the burnt-out club, raising his fist again in salute to the fallen.

Stormboy: AN-AR-CHY! OI OI OI OI!

              He and Davey exit. Julie is slumped down on the stairs. Terry stands, staring out.

Julie: What's the point? What's the bloody point? He's right. No point. No future.

Terry: These kids . . . It doesn't make sense. I can't make any sense of it.

              (*Stormboy*) He doesn't make sense!

              (*Oik*) Or him!

Julie: Terry – I can't take any more. I swear I can't.

Terry: (*oblivious; angry*) How dare they, Jools? How dare they – burn themselves up – throw themselves away! Like it was nothing. For nothing. When we – when we – !

Julie: Don't –

Terry: (*rounds on her*) When we can't have them! When we can't even have kids!

Julie: When I can't have them. Say it.

Terry: (*slowly*) When you can't have them. When you'll never have a baby.

The unsayable is finally said.

Julie: You had a test, didn't you?

Terry nods.

Terry: I couldn't tell you it wasn't me. I thought as long as there was doubt you'd have – a bit of hope.

Julie: I know what it means to you, Terry.

Terry: You don't. You only know what it means to you.

Julie: What does it mean? I want to know.

Terry looks at her a moment.

Terry: It's a failed expedition. It's Scott of the bloody Antarctic, isn't it? Everything. Emigrating. It was the right thing to do. We just can't finish the job.

Julie: Let me go, Terry. You're young enough – you could find someone else . . .

Terry: You're talking daft.

Julie: So we don't have the – pain – of having to look at each other every day.

Terry: I won't let you go.

Julie: For me. For me! So it's not raw on my nerves, doing my head in day-in day-out, every time I look at you. Don't you see? If it was just me, I could cope.

Terry comes to her, holds her.

Terry: I won't let you, Jools. If you sneak off, if you run away – I'll go after you. I'll bring you back. Hear me?

Julie starts to quietly cry. Terry looks up.

Terry: Sun's coming up.

Julie: Does that mean it's going down in London? I can't do the arithmetic no more.

Terry: I'm tough, Julie – hard as nails. You lean on me – and we do it together. Right?

Julie: Sod you, Terry. I'm catching the bus home.

Terry starts to quietly sing 'Waterloo Sunset' from the line about their namesakes.

Oh no, Terry . . .

He keeps singing.

That song's like a curse.

She continues to sob against him as he sings as far as the end of the verse.

The Kinks' version of the song comes up to take over as the lights slowly fade.

THE END

OUTTAKE

This is from a very early draft of Waterloo Sunset *– it's an 'outtake' as it didn't end up in the play. Originally I was thinking of bookending the play with an older Cat looking back. This would have been the speech that opened the play. I've always liked it but it didn't have a place in the produced play and had to stay in the bottom drawer. I see I called the character April then – so guess it should stay that way. I think she'd be in her thirties here, still punkish in appearance.*

April: This place isn't here any more. The whole thing burned – fell into the water. Street kids lighting fires. Only there was no such thing back then – 1980. No street kids – just punks. Skins. Boots. And Design students.

Sid Vicious was dead. And what would he have thought of this place if he wasn't? Not exactly the Chelsea Hotel. More the Rovers Return. Would he have seen the funny side? I didn't think about it too much – just sat here when we came here, wide-eyed beside my man my boyfriend my one and only, saying nothing – out of shyness, and not knowing how to be cool here, and because of the wooden block the scrumpy turned my tongue into and my brain into, until I slid off my chair and had to be escorted home by my chivalrous man and all his punk brothers. Pausing by Roy's Burger Bar for the most acidic puke that ever brought blood to my throat and tears to my little girly eyes.

I didn't know we had nowhere to go. I didn't know I should have really organised to be 16 three years before. 1977. When it wasn't on the chart but in the heart. That tight time when to shout 'Disco sucks!' wasn't a truism but a call to revolution. When it was new and it was ours and it was sweet in the mouth. But I hadn't been there. In '77 I was 13 in Lower Hutt. So this had to be my time.

I didn't know we were dying. All of us. I thought we were having the time of our lives.

My Dad used to talk about Poms. You know, the unions and stuff. Soon as someone on TV would open their mouth – 'bloody typical, have to be a Pom'. Here was the only place it wasn't a bad thing. Here it was a good thing to talk like Michael Caine and eat pickled eggs. It never occurred to me that half of them were putting it on. I never wondered – except maybe dimly through the scrumpy haze – what they were doing here when they so much wanted to be there. Enough to try to build an old boatshed into a little corner of England.

That's my last question – never asked then, and still unanswered. When we were in here, where were we? London, they told me – as the wind seemed to ripple the floorboards and the iron roof wrenched at its nails and the tide came in underneath us. 'London, love', leaning across the table through the smoke, so many ship's stewards and chippies and sparkies and their whippet wives with quintessentially British teeth, 'Can't you hear the double-decker buses and the pigeons and the sparrers and the barrers dahn the market, Portobello Road, Old Camden Town . . .' And I could. I could so long as fermented apple juice fizzed through my brain like mescaline, I could hear it all and more besides. Johnny Rotten's sing-song voice outside Buckingham Palace, the Clash and the Damned pogoing it up at the Notting Hill Carnival, a tide of spikes and pins and boots bobbing down the King's Road, Malcolm McLaren whistling 'Anarchy in the UK' as me and my boy cross the street, slouching towards his Sex shop to be born.